Shut Up and Listen

Shut Up and Listen

Communication with Impact

Theo Theobald
&
Cary Cooper

Pro Vice Chancellor (External Relations) and
Professor of Organizational Psychology and Health, Lancaster University

palgrave
macmillan

First published 2012 by
PALGRAVE MACMILLAN

Palgrave Macmillan in the UK is an imprint of Macmillan Publishers Limited, registered in England, company number 785998, of Houndmills, Basingstoke, Hampshire RG21 6XS.

Palgrave Macmillan in the US is a division of St Martin's Press LLC, 175 Fifth Avenue, New York, NY 10010.

Palgrave Macmillan is the global academic imprint of the above companies and has companies and representatives throughout the world.

Palgrave® and Macmillan® are registered trademarks in the United States, the United Kingdom, Europe and other countries

ISBN-13: 978-0-230-31427-6

This book is printed on paper suitable for recycling and made from fully managed and sustained forest sources. Logging, pulping and manufacturing processes are expected to conform to the environmental regulations of the country of origin.

A catalogue record for this book is available from the British Library.

A catalogue record for this book is available from the Library of Congress.

10   9   8   7   6   5   4   3   2   1
21   20   19   18   17   16   15   14   13   12

Printed and bound in Great Britain by
MPG Group, Bodmin and King's Lynn

CONTENTS

If you're in a position where people are relying ever more heavily on your ability to articulate your ideas, marshal your resources and achieve your joint objectives then better communication is critical. Wouldn't it be good then, if you could learn the lessons of those who had gone before you, without having to go through the pain?

Amongst other things, this book contains the collected wisdom and experience of over a score of individuals who have become experts in communication, from business, academic life and beyond. We used their input to test the validity of many of the current ideas about effective communication. We wanted to be sure that this is how real people really communicate in real situations. Along the way, they shared with us interesting and unusual stories of their own communication styles, as well as considering what the future might hold in this technology driven medium.

As authors, our own communications experiences vary widely, which is something that has benefitted us both, even when we didn't necessarily agree about one aspect or another! Cary Cooper is a professor of Organisational Psychology who has spent his academic career studying and researching both the things that make us tick, like motivation, and, maybe more importantly, the things that don't, like stress. What has run through his study, as a common thread is the need for effective communication in the workplace.

Theo Theobald is an ex-advertising copywriter and former BBC executive who spent much of his career trying to solve the communications problems of his own organisation and other peoples'. Since turning freelance in 2001, he has continued to work with a wide variety of organisations, both as consultant and management trainer, and as an advisor on internal and external communications, including a number of high profile campaigns.

In coming together, to co-author this book, we hope to bridge the gap between rigorous academic study and the practicalities of life in today's workplace, giving you insight into what underpins great communications, as well as a host of great practical information, to help you deliver it.

During the research and writing phases, there were a number of surprising discoveries about some key aspects of communication. Perhaps the most intriguing paradox of all, is that despite the impact of technology, which has changed some communication channels out of all recognition there remains an astounding simplicity within the core principles, which have stayed the same for generations.

As we embarked on the process of updating the original work, it turned out our instincts were right. Since its first publication in 2004, the principles of *Shut up and Listen* have remained unchanged. Of course the world of communication devices and channels has altered almost beyond recognition. Back then none of us had heard of Twitter, 'social networking' had not been coined as a term and who would ever have dreamed of the iPad (except Steve Jobs, of course!).

This new edition includes insight into the changes, both from us and some new contributors. We also debate the impact of technology on the culture of communication, the rules may not have changed, but perhaps we are adapting to the devices and methods which are now available in a completely new way.

With all of the practical issues we cover, we've tried to take a step back to find what's really going on. So just what is the significance of email, what are the risks of text messaging, or even the expectations others might have of us when it comes to spelling, grammar and use of plain language?

Ultimately, we don't think that great communication is that difficult and yet despite that, an awful lot of people still seem to get it horribly wrong, you will find some interesting examples of this as you read through the text.

More than anything we hope you enjoy the book and benefit from communicating more effectively. We have done our best to write it in an accessible, conversational way, because, being true to the principles we champion later on, we believe this is the right tone for modern communicators.

How to enjoy this book

> *'It seems that if you get an organisation with more than about 7 people then lines of communication get extended and messages get confused'.*
> Michael Broadbent – HSBC

We are much better communicators when we **know** more about ourselves, **think** about how and what we communicate and **act** according to the changes in our circumstance and environment.

These are the main principles of the book. To make life easier up front, here is a shorthand road map of what is coming up. There are three main sections, starting with a short course in self awareness, giving you time and space to reflect on who you are, so you can find out more about your favoured communication style. It's a sense check of where you are now, which is really important, firstly, if you're going to better understand how your various 'audiences' see you, and secondly in deciding what, if any changes you want to make to the way you send and receive your communications.

The middle part of the book (the second and largest section) is all about 'how to...'

Lots of business books talk a lot about strategy (the plan), but leave you feeling hungry for tactics (the day to day things you have to do to implement it). We take it as read, that you have some kind of plan for your future and that in work, there are some expectations upon your shoulders, in terms of how you communicate, so all we're attempting to do here is give advice and offer you options on the best way to put it into practice.

There are five main subsections within 'how to' looking at reading, writing, listening, talking and feeling where you'll find tips on everything from how to persuade your boss to give you a company car, through to the best use of PowerPoint in a formal presentation. The tools and techniques are part of the story, but how you change your mind set and attitude to the way you communicate is equally important.

As well as the considerable contribution of our expert panel, which we gratefully acknowledge, we have added lots of our own case studies and stories collected during our careers in business and education. So we equally express our thanks to the many unsung heroes whose anecdotes and experiences help to consolidate the theoretical learning.

All that 'how to' advice is great, but what about getting started on the implementation? Help is at hand, towards the end of the book, in the third section, with a guide to planning which is simple enough to take the pain of the process away, but still effective enough to ensure you implement your own changes.

Features

That's the basic structure, but we've also included a number of features that complement the main text, which are explained below.

'According to...'

We conducted in depth interviews with experts, to get a wide range of input and opinion about the elements of effective communication, so throughout the book you'll find quotes taken from those discussions which support the theories.

Apart from top business leaders and academics we looked at communication in other spheres, such as medicine and politics, to see if the challenges were greater, or even just different, and if we could learn something that could be adapted to our work place.

A full list of the contributors can be found in Appendix II.

The Expert Panel

In addition to the short quotes that you find under the title of 'According to...' there are some more fully developed stories that stand-alone. These you'll find in separate panels of text, interwoven with the rest of the book.

Pearls of wisdom

During the course of the interviews our contributors sometimes came out with unmissable one-liners that summed up a particular aspect of communication. Where it's appropriate, we've applied them to particular sections of text to reinforce a point. There are definitely some that are worth committing to memory, for use at an apposite moment.

Short summaries

Some golden nuggets of information are priceless, but it's hard to remember huge passages of text, so, we've tried to capture our unforgettable gems in a short bullet point form.

Try this

Having a go at something new can be a great way of refreshing our outlook on a subject. There are lots of practical suggestions of things you can do to make your communication better. It's up to you how many you adopt, but don't be afraid to have a go, it might prompt you to think up your own list of things to try.

A Good Story

From time to time, we hear a tale which perfectly illustrates a business situation we've been in. Sometimes they're things that really happened and sometimes urban myth, but still with a relevance to the problems we face. Whether they are true is less important than whether they are memorable. We learn lots from stories, and by recalling their teaching, we can avoid pitfalls in future.

The Elevator Test

Top firms of consultants use this technique when they're working with their clients. They prepare themselves to report succinctly on progress at any time, by imagining they're caught in the elevator by the CEO and they have just a few floors to summarise where they're up to. We've applied a similar test at the end of each chapter to précis its contents. Each provides a snapshot of the preceding text.

Ready to start? Before we do, a final few words about the importance of communication. More than any other management discipline, this is the one we must get right. Whatever we are attempting to achieve, it cannot be done without clarity of thought and word. As the whole nature of work has changed from the days of a manufacturing economy, to a service led one, the thread which runs through all successful organisations and individuals is the ability to communicate effectively, succinctly, powerfully.

Beware too of those who use communication as a blunt instrument to de-rail your 'best laid plans'. The universally used excuse for any business ill is 'a breakdown in communication'. This can only ever happen if our 'sending' or 'receiving' is flawed. Sometimes it's good to remember we need to 'Shut up and Listen'.

SECTION 1
Insight

We're never too old or experienced to discover something new about the world, working life or ourselves

CHAPTER 1

Revelations

We begin with some fundamental principles which underpin communication. We have called them 'revelations', not because they have lay undiscovered until now, but due to the fact that 'raising consciousness' is one of the running themes of this subject. There are many aspects of business where we instinctively know the right thing to do, and yet problems and issues continue to arise because we fail to follow that instinct.

Going back to basics, gives us the opportunity to consider these core principles and think about how we can apply them on a daily basis to improve our communication. So, with the help of the experts, we will examine the role of the truth, the unfathomable quality called 'charisma, some characteristics of great communicators and the 'lessons from childhood' which we may have since unlearned.

Revelation 1 – Telling the truth

It seems odd to begin by talking about telling the truth, surely we all do that most of the time don't we? It appears in business this is not the case, there are versions of the truth which we bend this way and that, to satisfy our own needs, those of our customers or the organisation as a whole. We often have the best of motives when not being entirely truthful, but we need to understand that a lack of truth affects the clarity of our communication.

Allied to this term is 'trust'. For relationships to work effectively (in or out of work), we need to be able to trust each other. If the boss is duplicitous we are guarded, when a supplier breaks a promise we feel let down and a colleague who is two-faced is ostracised.

Good business practice relies on trust, and what is that without truth?

So we set out to get to the bottom of what the truth is in the workplace. It wasn't always easy. Not surprisingly we failed to uncover anyone who advocated lying as a way of getting on in business, but that didn't always mean people were entirely truthful in all their dealings.

What was interesting was the range of views about what constitutes the truth – it seems that getting the definitive version of the facts can sometimes be more complex than you might think.

Here are the views of a number of contributors to give you a balance of opinion to compare with your own.

We start, not in the world of business, but medicine, with Doug Simkiss a Consultant Paediatrician at the Birmingham Community Children's Centre.

'At diagnosis I don't hide behind terms like a growth or a nodule or something, if it's cancer, it's cancer, if it's cerebral palsy, it's cerebral palsy. I use the medical term because if you try and spare people the medical terms, they can't find any information afterwards, and anyway, if you don't use the proper terms someone else will, at some stage.

When it comes to the *whole* truth, in terms of the medical consequences of a condition, we're rubbish working that out at diagnosis anyway, because children are all different. You can use the same terms about a child, like cerebral palsy for example but the consequences can vary greatly.

So I guess I'd say we have to tell the truth as far as we know it, but the consequences become clearer over time, and there often has to be a re-adjustment of what the truth means'.

Telling the truth, as we know it, is very important, but even with the best of intentions, it might not be possible to explain the whole truth. In a medical situation, if we are diagnosed with something serious, we want to know the path ahead, what will the outcome be, what are the timescales, the chances of full recovery, the after effects of the illness? Even seasoned professionals like Doug are not able to accurately predict these things, because sometimes the truth relies on better data than we currently have. At best we are guessing on the basis of what has gone before. Medical professionals are often circumspect for these reasons.

In a business context we may also have good motives for not telling the whole story all of the time. There are occasions when the whole truth might be commercially sensitive or plain tactless, or you may encounter circumstances where people simply don't want to hear the truth, like in a redundancy situation.

Equally, the truth can be different according to where you're viewing it from. This is never more so than when two parties can't seem to compromise, each clinging dearly onto their version of events.

According to...

John Akers – Relationship Counsellor

'In Birmingham there's a telephone tower which we could see from our offices, so I used to say to people if you look at that tower from here you know exactly what it looks like, but if you look at it from somewhere else in Birmingham it's different, because there are different satellite dishes you can see, but it's still the same telephone tower.

And, in the same way, your perception of this situation that you're in now is different, because you are only looking at it from one place – the truth is we have a problem here, but what the *facts* are is very much harder to find out because it depends on which position you are viewing from'.

So the truth may be partly defined by your angle of vision, literally your point of view. Things get even more complicated sometimes and our next contributor believes there is an extra layer of complexity, he thinks the truth is contextual, that's to say it is of its time and place.

BACKGROUND

In the 1980s, Britain's political scene was dominated by the conservative party, under Margaret Thatcher. In a move against this, voters in Liverpool elected Derek Hatton, as deputy leader of the council. Hatton was not only a member of the Labour party, but also belonged to the leftwing Militant faction, which eventually brought him into dispute with his own party members as well as the ruling Conservatives.

According to…

Derek Hatton, Broadcaster and former Labour Politician

'People often say to me if you had your time over again would you do the same thing and I say if it was May 4th 1983, the day we took control, I wouldn't do a single thing different. If it was May 4th 2003 I wouldn't do a single thing the same.

It's not about truth, it's about what is relevant at that time, and at that time, there needed to be a passion, there needed to be an understanding of what was going on, there needed to be support around, you needed to know how to motivate that support. You needed to know how to mobilise that support, you needed to be absolutely committed to what you were saying, it was not a case of truth or non-truth, you can play games with that if you want, but it's really about context'.

Hatton is correct in one regard, we often re-write the truth of our history, not just in political terms, but as individuals. We may exaggerate our triumphs or disasters when we look at them retrospectively. Over time our nostalgia kicks in and the grass looks greener, the skies bluer when we look back, how hard is it then to get to the real truth?

In organisational terms, truth is desperately important. Integrity is one of the values espoused by many managers and appears in all the glossy corporate brochures, but it's something which must be lived, day-to-day, by everyone in the company, or it ceases to be credible.

Organisations now talk about their 'employee brand'. This is the version you will see in the recruitment pages, where they are trying to portray themselves as an employer of choice for prospective talent. Here, being truthful is critical as successful applicants, who have bought into the offer will eventually get to see 'below stairs', when they will make their own judgement over the truthfulness of the promises.

According to...

Lynn Rutter – Oxfam

'A lot of organisations haven't caught onto the need for honesty, they do this great external PR, put a lot of time and money into their advertising style and their brand image, and then on day one, the person starts and thinks "hang on a minute, this isn't what I thought, where's the company I joined?"'

In recent years, many large organisations have started to debate this issue by looking at the 'employee brand' of the organisation. What this means is that the workforce inside a company has a view of the values of the organisation, and increasingly the evidence points to a need to make this internal brand consistent with the consumer brand. So if your customers see you as standing for high ethical values, you must treat staff in a way which is consistent with this.

The days when organisations could say one thing and do another are long gone. The swell of support behind ethical issues, now under the broader banner of Corporate Social Responsibility, make it essential for brand values to be lived out on a daily basis.

So, what can we conclude about the truth? We have a medical man who thinks that it can vary according to individual circumstance, and a counsellor who believes that the angle of view changes the perspective. All of which is consolidated by the ex-politician who says that timing and context are paramount, plus a business leader who thinks that 'consistency' is the key.

So although degrees of truth may vary according to who you ask the question of, there is general agreement on one point, 'the truth matters' and never more so than when we are communicating. Consider this across the board from the things we say, to the more subliminal messages we give out where actions speak louder than words. Before we appear to be holier-than-thou on this issue, we should offer a word of warning via this salutary tale.

Getting the balance right

Honesty is a key plank of effective communication, but presenting a warts-and-all view of yourself at every opportunity is unlikely to endear you to everyone.

The most famous case of foot-in-mouth disease was that of jewellery tycoon Gerald Ratner, whose stores were once a feature of many British high streets. In 1991 he made a speech to the Institute of Directors and joked that one of his firm's products was 'total crap', before going on to boast that some of their earrings were 'cheaper than a prawn sandwich'.

Ratner mistakenly believed he was addressing a closed audience of his peers, not realising there were journalists present. His words had been intended to amuse the audience of well off business people (in which he succeeded), but in so doing, he was ridiculing the loyal customer base who bought his products. The journalists present picked up on the story and the company dropped in value by £500m.

According to...

Keith Harris – Seymour Pierce

'Forget about the damage to the business, it was really about individuals who'd saved up to buy something from his shop, to give to somebody with all their heart and that was the real damage – that was truly awful'.

Ratner made the big mistake of believing he was simply talking to an audience of his peers, not realising there were journalists in the room. An added lesson from this story is the requirement in public to treat everything we say as 'on-the-record'. The advice given to many rising stars of the entertainment world is 'remember, every time you step out of your front door, you're on stage'. Whatever our business profile, it is advice worth heeding.

As technology has moved on, now everyone is a potential journalist, with a recording device and camera as standard on every mobile phone. Politicians and pop stars alike have since been 'caught' in similar unguarded moments.

Revelation 2 – The definition of charisma

> *'It's not all down to your natural personality because personalities don't change. I'm very clear that you can improve communication skills'.*
> Professor Chris Brewster

The possibility that great communicators possess a mystical quality called 'charisma', is really quite scary. After all, if they have it and we don't, then how can we ever be like them? In the spirit of busting some of the myths that surround communication, we chose to examine the issue of charisma in some more detail.

To the rescue came a number of authoritative figures who themselves excel in the art of communication. We start with a University professor.

According to...

Professor Chris Brewster

'I am extremely personally suspicious of words like "charisma", first of all because I don't know what it means and, secondly, because you might look at someone and say they've got great charisma, and I'd say they look really boring, so I think the whole concept is flawed.

I don't dismiss the importance of other traits, like "empathy" and a kind of understanding of where your audience is coming from'.

As John Akers said earlier, when talking about truth, it depends on where you are looking at if from, so it appears charisma is a similar thing, we don't all interpret it in the same way.

We stay in the academic arena for another view that helps to reinforce what Professor Chris Brewster thinks.

The Expert Panel

Professor David Clutterbuck

'When it comes to charisma, I was told that originally it meant "caring". It seems to me to have the ability to project the fact that you care is really important – so all those words like passion are replaced by that.

We think, 'does this guy know what he's talking about, and does he care about the subject?' If you do then you'll get people's attention, but if either of those two things is missing then you won't.

I think that what you see as charisma is driven by those two things. There are people who are good actors, but mostly the people who communicate well are those who care and the passion that you see is just an external expression of what's going on inside them.

We did some work and found a number of organisations were concerned about the way people were appraised on their verbal communication skills.

It was the area where people most often disagreed with how they were appraised, so we did some focus groups (with Birkbeck College), and found the assumption that good verbal communication is just related to personality is bunk. It is, of course, partly related to that, but many other factors come in.

"Awareness of context" is fundamental, as is "speed of communication", for example, if you put a Finn and a Columbian together they're going to struggle, because one speaks very slowly and the other very quickly.

So the critical quality of a good communicator is the ability to adapt to the other person you're working with. Whatever the message, you have to structure it around the other person's ability to receive'.

The really good news about charisma is that we don't have to try and seek it out as a holy grail, nor do we have to emulate the people who supposedly have it. In fact, it may be that there are elements of it we can develop over time, according to our circumstances and status. By concentrating on the elements outlined by Professor David Clutterbuck, like caring and empathy, we should become better communicators. Beyond that, people may begin to attribute charisma to us. Our next expert agrees.

According to...

Derek Hatton – Broadcaster and former Politician

'David Beckham appears on television around the world with the most unbelievable amount of charisma, he's a working class kid, he's not the most articulate of blokes, there's nothing special about him but because of the way he's been built up, all of a sudden charisma oozes out of him. So I don't think it's necessarily what you've got, sometimes it's what other people give you.

Okay, there are people that are born with it, there are people that naturally have it, they ooze that self-confidence and passion and everything that goes with it. I don't believe however, that's the only form of charisma you can have, I think there are many forms of charisma that you can actually acquire, or other people can acquire for you'.

We asked some experts of their view on charisma, as it seemed an important character trait of the universally recognised great communicators. A bit like 'culture', charisma seems to be one of those things which we all understand, but none of us is able to pin down very accurately, it's a kind of 'I know it when I see it' phenomenon.

The difficulty from the point of view of improving our personal communications, is that if we can't define charisma properly, then it's going to be even harder to try and emulate it. We've attempted to stay grounded and come up with a set of words that we can understand and aspire to, something which in a more definable way will eventually make us more charismatic. However, it seems the most important thing is to rely on getting the basics right, to attempt to really connect with the people we are talking to, after that we can let the bestowing of charisma upon us be the job of those we talk to.

Revelation 3 – Great communication characteristics

If we are ill at ease with these attempts to define charisma we need to find something to replace it with, something we feel is tangible. What then are the character traits which form the personality of a great communicator? When groups of managers are asked this question, time and again they come up with the same types of attributes, which are detailed below:

• Self-awareness
• Empathy
• Wit
• Passion
• Spark

These are the personal qualities which 'followers' revere, so let us examine them in a bit more detail.

Self-awareness – It's long been thought that the measure of ability in the form of I.Q. was a rather limited way of summing up a person. We probably all knew the brainy kid at school who never went on to do much in later life. Alternatively maybe the creative (but less academic) kid became a great designer or had a gift for teaching autistic children. Conventional cerebral intelligence isn't the only important quality in life.

Daniel Goleman (Author of Emotional Intelligence: Why it can matter more than I.Q. 1996), pioneered the measure of emotional intelligence, or E.Q., and many have followed since, reinforcing the theory that part of what makes us capable individuals is how 'in touch' we are with our emotions.

A key part of this is our ability to look at ourselves and understand how the world sees us. How do our actions and emotions impact on the people we interact with? What response might we expect from them in return? Great communicators think about this all the time. Improving our emotional intelligence can simply be a matter of taking the time to reflect a little more often and a little more deeply.

If our communication has resulted in conflict, it is worth considering why that may have been. A good way of doing this is to think about the situation as objectively as you can, from the point of view of the other party, then try to match this up with the way you saw things. Finally, imagine yourself as a third party to the dispute and contemplate the issue from this standpoint. Then, and only then, do we have the opportunity of understanding why our communication had the impact it did in some kind of objective sense.

Empathy – This key ingredient will turn up as a running theme in the following pages. It's about being able to see the world through the eyes of your audience, even if on the surface you have nothing in common with them. If you can't see what they see, you'll never be able to engage with them. Great communicators do this intuitively. Here's an example.

Charles is 52, and Managing Director of a large financial institution. His workforce is predominantly female aged 18 to 40. At the younger end of the spectrum are school leavers in their first junior role. The more mature workers include long serving staff many who are returning to work after maternity leave.

It would appear that Charles shares little common ground with either group, so how does he create empathy?

'I listen. As often as I can, I listen "one to one" rather than in groups, and I try not to conclude that everyone is like this individual. However, the more "one to one" listening I do, the more I can start to spot emerging trends. You have to see the whole person, not just the employee. We've offered cheaper mortgages to staff, helping the younger ones get on the first rung of the property ladder and flexible hours to ease the problems of childcare for the mums. These are the issues that concern them, you have to understand that'.

You don't have to be the *same* as the group you're trying to empathise with, but you do have to see *their* point of view.

<u>Wit</u> – We mean this in the widest sense of the word. It's not just about being funny (although that can be a big part of successful communication), but think of it also in terms of sayings like 'he had his wits about him', 'her response was very quick-witted'. In fact, wit is about having the ability to say or write things that are both amusing and clever, the ability to think quickly and clearly and make good decisions. And let's face it, there are times when we'd all like a bit more of that.

Humour is without doubt a double-edged sword, use it well and you will display an incisive ability to drive your message home; badly, and you could end up scarred for life! However, being quick-witted, (i.e. able to respond swiftly to any given situation) will stand you in good stead and make you a better communicator.

<u>Passion</u> – There is no replacement for passion and you can't manufacture it. Passion is driven by belief and faith; it's at our very core and it is one of the most powerful communications tools there is. Even when we vehemently disagree with someone's point of view, we will respect them enough to listen if they show real passion. The same is true for us, when we really feel strongly about a topic, it shows.

Think of something you feel passionate about, then imagine having to speak on the subject for a few minutes. How do you think you would look? How would you come across to your audience? If challenged on your beliefs, would you shrink back and concede? Or would you defend your position with vigour?

Now you can start to see how great communicators are able to inspire their audiences with the passion they feel for their subject.

Spark – first we ruled out 'charisma' as being too hard to pin down, now we're going to compromise by offering you 'spark' as an alternative. We are simply trying to convey the look that some people have which sets them apart, that makes us want to get to know them. Below is a list of descriptors that begin to define what we think 'spark' is.

Animated
Alive
Aware
Vibrant
Smiling
Enthusiastic
Lively
Energetic

Perhaps people with spark have better, happier, more fulfilled lives than the rest of us, but it's more likely that they have simply developed a confidence in what they are saying, which comes across in 'the way that they say it', 'the way they look' and 'the way they act'.

So these are what we believe are the important characteristics of great communicators, the question is, how much are we born with and how much do we learn. It's the age old nature/nurture debate. Like eye colour or height, some traits will be inherited, but heredity is only part of the story; environment, the way we were brought up, our childhood experiences are all part of who we are now. We learn certain behaviours, most importantly, we come to understand that we can go on learning, growing and gaining in experience. This is good news if we are to become better at communication.

Along the way though, we may forget some things. In adult life, we adopt certain ways of acting which are considered appropriate simply because they are 'grown up'. But perhaps there are things we have left behind which might still be useful.

Can we re-learn the lessons of our childhood?

Revelation 4 – Children – they know more than you think!

'Children are inclined to be direct, they don't beat about the bush, they're much more likely to say, "I don't want this!"'

John Akers – Relationship Counsellor

We started acquiring our communication skills a long time ago. In fact, we have already learned a lot to get to where we are now. Sadly, we've forgotten a lot too, and some of which would be really useful. Let's start by looking at what we might have to re-learn.

'I think children are more direct, more open and frank, and what can happen as we get older is that we behave according to the norms which may make us less direct and it's good to be reminded that direct communication is often the best, being frank, being succinct, being short and just telling it like it is'.

Val Gooding – BUPA

As adults we tend to take much more account of other peoples' feelings, we're sensitive to the environment we're operating in and aware of the subtleties of what is acceptable and what is not. Sometimes though this can work against us in achieving the things we want. In business, it can lead to an 'Emperor's new clothes' syndrome, particularly when the boss is aggressive and autocratic.

You reach a stage where everyone can see what's wrong but no one is prepared to question it. Being the little boy, who stands up, points his finger and says, 'you're naked!' can be a liberating experience.

There is a health warning with all this, because sometimes you can liberate yourself right out of the organisation altogether, so tread carefully and choose your moment!

According to...

Alistair Smith – Alite

'There's certainly a lot that good communicators do that emulates what children do, to learn naturally. The research, whether into primates or the structure of the brain, points to certain natural ways of learning and includes things like "imitation", "safe rehearsal" (without fear of recrimination), and "exploration", so you explore territory, you explore behaviours, you explore relationships.

The great thing about children is their "openness", which allows them to do things like "suspend politeness", and it's only when you suspend politeness that you can ask the disturbing question.

You'll get audiences with whom you're communicating, who will nod their heads and you'll think you're being very effective, but they'll leave you and go on doing and thinking what they were before and it's only when you've created relationships with them and asked the disturbing question that you'll make progress. Children do it habitually, and it's very powerful.

The other question children ask that good communicators ask is the "so what?" question, "this is all very well but what's it got to do with me? As a result of listening to you why am I better off?"

So for a communicator I think it's really important to acknowledge the significance of the "so what?" question. It's a great sense check and it's the reason why in advertising they continually think about selling the benefits, rather than just talking about the facts'.

Here is a summary of what we might have forgotten:

Be direct and open
Keep it short
Ask the disturbing question
Ask 'so what?'
Turn facts into benefits

We have tended to concentrate so far on the 'outbound communication' we undertook as children, the 'what' and 'how' of letting others know our thoughts and feelings. Now let's take a look at how we handled the information coming into us, how we received and how we learned.

Revelation 5 – The power of storytelling

'The best stories are universal and really skilled story-tellers have the ability to embed their message'.
Alistair Smith – Alite

The significance of storytelling is being recognised more and more in business, when it comes to making our messages engaging and memorable. Over recent years the fixation has been upon technology, the hardware which has increased our channels of communication, rather than the messages themselves and how they relate to their audience.

We've all sat back and marvelled at the latest invention, and the degree to which computer memory has fallen in price which has enabled the growth in mobile broadband. Mobile phones have long since reached market saturation, we see old people at bus stops texting or phoning, and at the early adopter end of the market, mobile internet has become an essential. Improvements in touch screen technology have resulted in a whole range of new tablets, pioneered by the iPad and now people can 'carry their world in their hand'.

In that environment, we may have forgotten some of the simpler things in life that have had and always will have a massive impact on what we teach and learn, irrespective of how the messages are sent from one party to the other.

One of the key elements of our learning is 'storytelling'. When we're very young, it is still one of the primary ways we find out about the world. Here we discover about values and morals, we are taught right from wrong.

The Expert Panel

Alistair Smith

Alite

'Every culture, every civilisation expresses itself through stories, and stories are metaphors for how we live our lives, what should be of significance and value in our lives. It's how one generation translates its wisdom to another.

A thousand years ago, it was camp fire stuff and I guess the story tellers back then were skilled at holding the attention, creating characters, embedding the key points, activating the significant learning later and giving you a sense of closure when it was all done.

As for the media, well, they're just electronic stories'.

Getting the people you work with to remember a certain point can be effectively executed through good storytelling, but raising the profile of a particular issue to a wider audience can also happen much more effectively. On one level it is a great vehicle for cascading a message within the organisation, but sometimes, if you have the right story, if it's interesting enough, it will attract outside interest too.

This is how good PR starts.

Here's a real life example to illustrate the point.

This story comes from the BBC's Head of Internal Communications, Russell Grossman.

The shock tactics in this story are part of what gives it its impact; add to that the memorable phrase 'BAFTA bastard', which conjures up an instant picture of the talented but difficult prima donna and it becomes even more impactful. This is all part of characterisation and the best stories need heroes and villains. The point of the story is both well made and memorable.

The Expert Panel

Russell Grossman
BBC

'I try to find particular examples and stories that people can relate to personally. So, for example, we wanted to get across the idea that bullying is out of the question.

There's a real problem in News and Current affairs with bullying, and it partly comes with the territory, because you've got hard pressure deadlines and you've got people who are hard bitten.

If you go into a newsroom, you have people shouting at each other, shouting instructions and if it doesn't get done on time they are verbally abused. That's not on.

The best way for us to get this across was to tell a story by a person who was most involved with it, and we got somebody who was quite happy to say "I'm the result of what we call BAFTA bastards, that's somebody who is recognised as great by the industry because they get a BAFTA, but actually back in the office they're an absolute bastard".

And the fact that we did it that way meant that the story was reported in Broadcast magazine, The London Evening Standard and The Times.

My point is that if we'd just said that bullying is no good, it just wouldn't have made the same impact'.

There may be other occasions when you're not trying to make it into the daily papers, but are attempting to make your point more memorable. The trick is to make the story relevant to the point you're trying to get across, something that illustrates it in a vivid way in people's minds. Great stories paint fantastic pictures.

According to…

> Lynn Rutter – Oxfam
>
> 'There's no point in standing up and giving a presentation in a way that the people aren't going to understand and, let's face it, glorious PowerPoint slides have their limitations.
>
> If you can't keep their attention and you can't tell stories you'll struggle, so I learned to tell stories and talk in a way that people could relate to, so yes, it is something that I work at all the time.
>
> They don't need to be stories that are related to work, they can be just "life stories", and if you tell a few that make fun of yourself that helps too.
>
> So I try to think of funny stories that people will remember, so that they'll then remember the bigger point behind it'.

In fact, Lynn Rutter is an excellent storyteller, and to prove the point we have included one of her anecdotes in the section on culture and environment.

Where appropriate, try to think of your communications as a one person PR campaign. How can you package your message in a way which people will relate to, is there a story which helps to illustrate your point and make it more memorable?

Try this

Start to collect stories.

When you hear a great tale, make a note of it and try to think through what it was that you liked about it. What 'learning points' did it make, can you re-apply that to a situation you'd like to teach to others?

Stories are often most powerful when they are about the person who is relating them, so think if you've been in a similar situation to the one in the tale and keep it personal. Don't stretch the truth too much, and remember that it is sometimes better to credit the original storyteller.

What are the funny things that happen to you? Have you ever locked yourself out? Lost your car in a large car park? Made a terrible social gaffe?

What did you learn from that experience, and can you relate it to something you'd like others to know? Particularly when we are in a position of authority, it does no harm to show some frailty, it makes us more credible and believable to our audience, more human.

What's so good about 'stories'? Here's a reminder.

A great way to illustrate a point
Often common across all cultures
High impact – very memorable
A trigger for more serious learning
Good way of building rapport

We are an amalgam of our experiences and learning, each having had a unique set of variables which coalesce into the person we are today. This is a great asset in communicating effectively, because one of the universal truths of life is we are all interested in people. If we communicate in the right way, our audience will be interested in us!

To build on this and really make the most of it, it helps greatly if we know ourselves better and there are some exercises coming up which might help with this. Before that, let us just clear the decks with some issues which may sound familiar. Let us examine some of the difficulties we all face when communicating.

Revelation 6 – Some common communication issues

'Most people can do most things if they put their minds to it, it's just about believing'.
Derek Hatton – Broadcaster and former Politician

That's a quote worth remembering when you come up against the inevitable communication problems you'll encounter.

One such issue is what we will define as 'wilful misunderstanding', a situation where you know the other party clearly knows your intention, but pretends otherwise for their own ends. This happens because there are some messages people don't want to hear and, under those circumstances, it's very difficult, if not impossible, to connect with them.

According to...

Professor David Clutterbuck

'If people don't like the message they tend to ignore it.

I recall one factory where they did just about everything they could think of to *hint* that the place was going to close, even to the point of measuring up the floor while the staff were working. When it was finally announced, the workforce went on strike, saying they didn't have a clue. People only hear messages that they are attuned to and want to hear.

If a message is unpalatable, we tend to tune it out, and our receptivity is affected by all sorts of factors. It can be about state of mind, about willingness to accept a message; it can be our perception of the person providing the data. If it comes from a source you don't believe to be credible, then you will probably be unreceptive, you won't take it in, especially if the message is contradictory to the basic judgments you have made about that individual or that organisation'.

This view is supported by Derek Hatton, a militant political leader of 1980s Britain, whose views were directly opposed to the Prime Minister of the day Margaret Thatcher.

According to...

Derek Hatton – Broadcaster and former Politician

'I could say that someone like Margaret Thatcher was a good communicator, but that would be very difficult. The times that I met her that I found she was a poor communicator because she was saying exactly the opposite of what I wanted to hear, and I suppose she would have said I was a poor communicator because I was saying exactly the opposite of what she wanted to hear'.

One of the more difficult aspects of managing people is that sometimes you have to be the bearer of bad tidings. If they aren't receptive to that, then it will always be tough. This issue is at the heart of one of management's most difficult tasks, handling conflict.

How to break the bad news
Being hesitant or vague, not coming straight to the point or dressing the message up in some way, can just make matters worse. These are the times when you simply have to tell it like it is.

For an expert view on the best way of doing this we asked Consultant Paediatrician Doug Simkiss, to talk about his golden rules for delivering bad news, bearing in mind this can sometimes mean delivering very difficult messages.

The Expert Panel

Doug Simkiss
Consultant Paediatrician

'I always make sure I can tell both parents together, and that I'll have enough time, free of interruptions to both talk and listen.

After that I do my best to work out where they are and what their understanding of the current predicament is, and finally, I try to be ruthlessly honest.

People respond to integrity, and if the story is straight. I find that it really helps to establish relationships, because sometimes these relationships are going to go on for 10 or 15 years, so it's important to reach a mutual understanding and respect for each other.

You have to ensure that people have plenty of opportunity to ask questions on the day, and you agree a date for a very early review where you'll sit down face to face again'.

In a business situation (where whatever news you're delivering is not a matter of life and death), there are things Doug Simkiss does which can be applied:

If it affects a group of people try and tell them together
Try to find out what, if anything, their current understanding is
Allow enough time
Ensure there is an opportunity to talk and listen
Expect to have to answer questions
Be honest – make sure you have your story straight

Doug Simkiss added that a colleague has started to make audio recordings of some of these difficult consultations, so that the sometimes shell-shocked recipients of the bad news can listen back carefully to what has been said later. It would be a good idea to at least have some accompanying written notes or answers to frequently asked questions to take away.

Setting a formal time for a further review meeting, and making clear what your availability is in the meantime can also help the process.

When it comes to delivering bad news, there is further advice from Kevin Roberts, CEO of Saatchi and Saatchi Worldwide, who says, 'the key rule of communication is you must deliver good news in writing in whatever form that takes, whether that's email or twitter or whatever and bad news must always be delivered face to face'.

Certainly the process of thinking through your communication in advance will be a great help. This is especially important if you have bad news to deliver or a potential conflict brewing, these are not situations where you want to be 'flying blind'. Try to anticipate how the other party will feel and come up with answers in advance which cover a variety of scenarios. You will appear much more self assured, and this confidence translates itself to the other party.

Many of these 'revelations' are common sense elements of communication. However, judging by the amount of poor com-munication that happens in organisations, it is always worth reminding ourselves of the basics. If we keep these issues at the forefront of our thinking, it is much more likely we will deliver our messages effectively and unambiguously, resulting in far fewer 'breakdowns in communication'.

The Elevator Test for Chapter 1

- The truth is important – be careful how you use it

- Sometimes, how much honesty you employ is affected by timing

- The term 'charisma' is subjective. It's related to caring, empathy, spark and wit

- Passion is a critical element of all truly effective communication

- Remember your childhood and be direct, open and frank, (appropriate to the culture you're working in)

- Storytelling is effective, the more so when it's relevant, personal and witty

- If you have bad news, deliver it with integrity and honesty. Deliver it face to face.

CHAPTER 2

What kind of communicator are you?

We have stressed the importance of self-awareness, it is an aspect of management which is often overlooked, but in seeing ourselves as others see us, we have the opportunity to adapt our behaviour to fit any given situation. Take every opportunity which is offered to increase your self-knowledge. Many organisations set up 360° feedback mechanisms as part of their performance management process. Beyond this, we have plenty of occasions when we can seek feedback from others and we should never underestimate the benefit of reflective thinking, something which is easy to do, if we simply make the time.

To add to your overall picture of who you are and how you operate, this chapter contains some self-assessment tools, to help consolidate the process of reflection and add another dimension to your thinking.

Before you undertake the task of assessing your own communication style, have a look at the types we've defined below. How many of them do you recognise? Do you fit into any of these categories, or do you display some of the characteristics of more than one? There is good and bad in each so try and capitalise on the positive aspects of the character types and steer clear of their shortcomings.

Try to think of at least one person you know who fits each description.

The secret agent

Play their cards close to their chest (too close sometimes). Treats the most insignificant of facts as confidential, especially if a superior has entrusted them with it.

Good news

Reliable, discreet, trustworthy.

Bad news

Staff confusion, breeds a suspicion culture, can be guilty of starting rumours.

The double agent

Feigns discretion, but has a foot in another camp. May sometimes be on your side, but you'll never be sure (until you feel the knife in your back!)

Good news

Is a useful ally in the short term, especially in a competitive environment.

Bad news

Is likely to be judged as untrustworthy in the long term, and quickly becomes dispensable.

The gossip columnist

Collects tittle-tattle, or when all else fails makes it up. Believes the definition of confidentiality is 'tell one other person'.

Good news

Has lots of 'friends', as everyone is willing to take the time to listen to the latest bit of scandal.

Bad news

Lacks credibility and is unlikely to be trusted by colleagues.

The dictator

Listens to no one, makes snap judgements and decisions and tells it like it is or how they believe it is.

Good news

Extremely clear in terms of direction and focus.

Bad news

Resentment builds when people think their views aren't being listened to.

The kitchen sink

Tells everyone everything, even if it's not relevant to the topic in hand.

Good news

Can never be accused of not keeping people informed.

Bad news

Bores you to death, no focus on the task in hand, wastes vast amounts of time going round the houses.

The mouse

Has an opinion on many important issues but lacks the self-confidence or ability to express it.

Good news

Astute, knows what is going on, may be seen as a good sounding board by others.

Bad news

Lacks the ability to influence because of fear of speaking their mind.

The exercise of outlining these different types is not so we can categorise everyone we know, but to highlight the character traits of different people with regard to their communication. It is also useful in 'holding up a mirror' to our own style. It helps to know that by acting in a certain way, there will be certain benefits, but there may be a corresponding counterpoint, something our colleagues would be less enamoured with.

Use this as a barometer of your personal preference, and add it to your self-awareness along with the results of the following communications effectiveness questionnaire.

Self-assessment – just how good a communicator are you?

Read through the following questions and note down which answer, a, b, or c, which most often applies to you. Don't take too much time over each question, instead, use your instinct to give the most honest answer you can. When you have completed all the questions, there is a marking scheme and some pointers, according to how you have scored.

1. When another person is talking to you, you tend to:
    a. devote your entire attention to them
    b. listen to them but your mind wanders from time to time
    c. rarely listen with a great deal of 'mind wandering'

2. When presenting a case, you tend to:

   a. ensure the people listening are given ample opportunity to intervene during your presentation
   b. sometimes allow people to intervene when you notice they want to
   c. like to finish before taking any questions or clarifications

3. In trying to convince somebody to do something, you tend to:

   a. present only rational arguments
   b. present rational arguments but use some emotional messages
   c. appeal to them on an emotional level

4. Before communicating an important message to people at work, you tend to:

   a. plan thoroughly what you are going to say
   b. think through what you are going to say but not plan it precisely
   c. do little planning, go with the flow and communicate in the here-and-now

5. If somebody in your team had not performed well on a particular job, would you:

   a. be fairly assertive and direct about their performance
   b. try to communicate the problem calmly but also with some assertiveness
   c. try to support the person and let them know what they did that was wrong

6. If you had to dismiss someone at work would you:

   a. let the personnel officer do it
   b. leave most of the responsibility with personnel but offer the opportunity for discussion with you
   c. see them face-to-face

7. When you arrive at work do you tend to:

    a. plan all your communications by listing the meetings, emails and calls you need to make
    b. respond to what comes in throughout the day
    c. do some planning but build in a contingency for unexpected incoming tasks

8. Do you view text messaging as:

    a. a way of keeping in touch with friends to make social arrangements
    b. the primary method of keeping your colleagues updated
    c. a way of alerting workmates to important news

9. Do you think the use of good spelling and grammar is:

    a. a must-have tool in the communications mix
    b. an outdated concept as communication is now less formal
    c. a nice-to-have, but not essential

10. In important decision-making meetings do you tend to:

    a. talk more than you listen
    b. listen more than you talk
    c. do both in equal measure

How did you score?

Question 1. a = 3, b = 2, c = 1
Question 2. a = 2, b = 3, c = 1
Question 3. a = 1, b = 3, c = 2
Question 4. a = 3, b = 2, c = 1
Question 5. a = 2, b = 3, c = 1
Question 6. a = 1, b = 2, c = 3
Question 7. a = 2, b = 1, c = 3
Question 8. a = 2, b = 1, c = 3
Question 9. a = 3, b = 1, c = 2
Question 10. a = 1, b = 3, c = 2

What your score means

21–30
You are already a good communicator, thoughtful, passionate and prepared to listen. You take time to consider how the other party is feeling and are committed to continually improving your communication, both in terms of its style, and your command of new technologies.

You may sometimes find it hard to balance your I.Q (intelligence) with your E.Q. (emotions) in choosing whether to present bare facts, or the passion you feel about the subject.

11–20
You have a good instinct for communication, which will serve you well in most business situations. Most of the time you are fairly well planned, take time to think about what you are portraying to others and are assertive in your actions.

Occasionally you may feel you have not presented your best side, or may have failed to justify your arguments because you have not had sufficient time to think them through.

1–10
Although you understand the basics of communication you need to take some time fine-tuning your style. You feel there are too many occasions when other people don't seem to understand your point, or take up a contrary stance for no good reason.

You may often get bogged down with information overload, and need to find ways of filtering incoming messages to free up more time. It might be that you are not making the best use of the available technology and could do with brushing up on tools and techniques.

Developing self-awareness is best done across a range of tools and exercises, so the next one is designed to give you the opportunity to take a good hard look at the kind of impression you currently make on other people, especially at a first meeting.

Choose one from each of the three columns below that best describes how you believe other people see you.

SOCIAL SKILL	BUSINESS SKILL	ATTITUDE
Warm	Efficient	A doer
Outgoing	Demanding	A thinker
Engaging	Scatty	Aggressive
Witty	Smart	Submissive
Cold	Energetic	Cool
Stand-offish	Focussed	Approachable
Shy	Rigorous	Empathetic
Measured	Effective	Understanding
Extrovert	Demanding	Pragmatic
Gregarious	Creative	Friendly
Reserved	Fastidious	Weak
Friendly	Decisive	Familiar
Cautious	Active	Collaborative

Now think of where you would *like* to be. Consider this in terms of a person who might have impressed you on first meeting. What was it about him or her that gave you the 'wow' factor? Was it their status, the way they looked, a confident handshake, wit, a self-deprecating air, charm, what they said or the way that they said it?

One stage further

As it is, this exercise is a useful way of working out the kind of communicator you are. If however, you want an even more objective view, show the list to a couple of your peers and ask them to pick the three words they think sum you up best. The truth will probably be a mix of all the results.

Where do you want to be?

This final exercise is designed to flesh out your existing perception and consider a target for the future, something to aspire to.

Look at the 'word pool' below and answer both questions separately, by selecting just five words from the pool. You can have as much or as little cross-over, between your two lists, as you want, but be as honest as you can. It's much easier if you start by picking all the words in the pool that apply to each answer, and then filter it down to your final five.

Q1. How do you see yourself?

Q2. What other characteristics would you most like to have?

The word pool

professional, caring, self-reliant, tough, honest, effective, efficient, tenacious uncompromising, loyal, aggressive, creative, talented, knowledgeable, serious, outgoing, popular, determined, visionary, shy, amusing, cerebral, diligent, fastidious, industrious, helpful, conscientious, faithful, hardworking, ambitious, humorous, easy-going, credible, deep, intelligent, far sighted, empathetic

There are two interesting aspects to this exercise; the first is in what we hone our final choice down to. Bearing in mind we may initially have come up with 15 or 20 words, the need to prioritise helps to focus our attention on what we believe to be *really* important. The second factor is the transfer of words in and out of the pool, as the second question is answered.

At the end of this process you will have five words that describe how you want to be perceived in future and the kind of value system you wish to project.

What you have now done is to raise your level of consciousness about who you are and how you want to be perceived, the implementation of this in a variety of communication situations is easy, as long as you keep these adjectives in mind.

How to become more confident

Great communication is a question of confidence. Often our outward appearance can mask our inner feelings.

Andy's presentation

Andy had just been promoted and had to give his first presentation to the senior management team. He prepared well, rehearsing the material frequently. A colleague had even gone through his PowerPoint slides with him as a double check. On the day, he delivered the presentation very well and afterwards his boss, who had been in the audience, took him to one side to congratulate him.

Andy confessed, 'I was really nervous' at which his boss surprised him and said 'Well, if that's true you hid it very well, it didn't show at all'.

This sort of conversation is common in business and the important thing to learn is that often it's not how you feel inside, but how you project that is important. With face-to-face presentations there is only one way to improve and that is to do more. Try to take every opportunity which comes your way to be up on your feet.

We soon come to realise that it is the 'appearance of confidence' which is important, it is what gives us authority. Conveniently, with practice this 'false confidence' we all sometimes feel, begins to become a reality, as we begin to conquer our nerves, be ourselves and let our natural passion for a subject shine through, the more you fake it at first, the less you will have to later.

So far we have mainly taken our own opinion of where we are, but it is obviously useful to get the input of other people, so that the picture becomes more objective and balanced.

We talked earlier about commonly used tools in performance appraisal, and said that more and more organisations are using 360° feedback where a much wider circle of people get to comment on how you perform. This will probably include your peers, customers, staff and yourself.

Almost without fail, we tend to mark ourselves lower than anyone else does because it is part of our culture to be self-effacing. This modesty is a good thing, but it does fight against self-confidence. Having other people tell you your performance is outstanding is a great boost and likely to make you raise your game even further.

This doesn't mean you have no faith in your own ability, you probably know the things you're good at, but still we can scarcely believe that other people see us as so capable. A lack of self-confidence is no respecter of rank, status, age or experience. In interviews we have conducted, we found leading academics who would quiver at the sight of a microphone pointed in their direction, articulate and inspirational business leaders who miraculously became tongue-tied when they knew we were recording the conversation.

It is our experience that everyone, regardless of status or authority, has some degree of self-doubt, some moment when they can't actually believe they've reached the position they now hold. If you look up enviously at some of these figures then take heart.

According to...

Professor Cary Cooper

'I should actually listen to broadcasts I make, but you know why I don't do it, I'm frightened that I'll hear that I'm not very good and undermine my self-confidence, isn't that the stupidest thing?

But it's an act of avoidance and I shouldn't do that really – I should listen to my radio broadcasts, watch my TV broadcasts and just see if I said silly things and what I can learn, but I'm frightened I'll think I'm so lousy, I won't go on again!'.

Even the seemingly self-assured performers have odd crisis of confidence.

According to...

Simon Terrington – Human Capital

'The thing is we're all just blagging it, aren't we? That's the whole point in life.

You know the syndrome most chief executives suffer from is called the "Outsider Syndrome", which is the fear that someone is going to tap you on the shoulder and say you've been found out, we know you've been bluffing the whole time, we know that you shouldn't really be doing this, you're not up to it. And everyone's afraid of that.

I think we have a culture of hero worship, because we believe that Chief Executives are these supermen and super-women who create empires. I always think that in any company no one knows all the answers, and once you realise that, it's actually very liberating'.

In the small hours of the morning, we can all lie awake worrying we are not much good, but remember, it's what *other* people see that matters. Instead of focussing on shortcomings, try instead to get an accurate picture of how good your communication is by seeking the opinion of others.

How to get feedback

Getting feedback on a regular basis about the way we appear to others is a vital part of self-development; really effective communicators do this all the time and it's not difficult to achieve.

The easiest way to find out is to ask. You don't have to make it look like you're fishing for compliments or unsure of your ground either. If it's a colleague, a peer or even one of your own staff, you can ask in an open and honest way, and you will usually get a frank and honest answer.

It's here that a 'mentor', either officially appointed or unofficially adopted, can be a great help. Mentors are usually people with more experience than you who operate at a senior level. They can use their hard won wisdom to advise and guide you. Another way of approaching this issue is to pair up with a peer mentor, someone of a similar level within the organisation who does a different job but understands your role. Under these circumstances you can agree to a reciprocal mentoring deal, using each other to bounce ideas off.

You can also involve others on an occasional basis, so you get a range of responses. For example, after a team briefing you might take one of your staff to one side and ask, 'How do you think the rest of the team will have received that information? Do you think what we're doing is clear? Is it fair? What problems do you think we might encounter?' They're sure to appreciate your honesty and feel good about you valuing their opinion and input.

Choose someone for your feedback who you trust. It also helps if they have a degree of sensitivity because some of the things they tell you will inevitably feel uncomfortable at first, but it's honesty you want, not verbal abuse.

Raising your level of consciousness about feedback can also help, because in a range of situations from one-to-one meetings through to formal presentations, you can start to observe your audience more critically for non-verbal signs of approval, or otherwise. We will examine this topic of non-verbal signals in more detail later.

According to...

Val Gooding – BUPA

'One vitally important piece of advice I'd offer is to ask more questions – it works in a huge range of situations. Maybe you're in a situation where you've been promoted to a new job and you're not sure what you should be doing. A lot of people will try and cover up that they're not sure of their ground and swan around looking supremely self confident. The best thing to do is ask questions whatever level you're at. Ask questions, be nosey, be curious and don't be deterred if you're asking a question of a very senior person, somebody more important than you. Keep asking questions, that's how you learn and become more effective'.

Try this

Record yourself

There is a range of voice recording devices available, but the simplest method is to use your mobile phone, most now have this feature built in. Using a voice recorder is a good way to capture your thoughts.

In future, you need not worry about having pen and paper to hand, you can still capture your thoughts quickly and review them later. You can do this during downtime, like during your daily commute, or when waiting for a meeting to start.

As well as recording your thoughts, which is great if you are a creative type who has lots of ideas, you can use your device as an aid to memory, or you can make lists of things you need to do or achieve.

If you have to make a speech or presentation you can dictate it and listen back until, through repetition, you have memorised it. If you are preparing for an interview, record your dummy questions and leave a pause before dictating the pre-prepared answer, then try to get as close to the original when you are listening back.

With the agreement of other parties, you can even record a meeting or presentation, and listen back to your performance later. If you have taken the advice of securing a mentor, you can listen back together and analyse your communication skills.

Don't be put off by the sound of your own voice, we all hate that at first, but pretty soon you get used to it and can begin to focus on the content of what you have said. In the beginning you might also cringe at your 'verbal ticks' a tendency to 'umm' and 'errr', but it is a good way of increasing self-awareness and once we know we do this, we can begin to concentrate harder on eliminating it and delivering in a more seamless, and confident way.

The Elevator Test for Chapter 2

- Most of us are a mixture of different communication types. We adapt our style according to surroundings

- Self-assessment exercises help us raise our consciousness. It's easier to see how other people view us

- We usually mark our own abilities below the level that others do

- Projecting confidence makes us appear more competent

- Seek feedback whenever possible, use a wide group of people and mix formal and casual methods

- Ask questions all the time, it's the best way to learn

How to...

The practical guide to much better communication

How to – Introduction

Now we have had the chance to look at the kind of communicator we are and think about how we might change in future. Down to earth practical advice is what is needed, often people try to overcomplicate their communication, the result is ambiguity and the repercussions can be difficult to deal with.

So, the following chapters deal with the real practical issues of how to communicate effectively using a variety of tools across a range of situations.

The 'how to' of great communication is easy as long as you stay conscious of the practical rules that govern it.

We begin with a section on how to handle different communication channels, when you're making contact for the first time. This is a critical part of establishing relationships, and first impressions matter. We will then group 'communication' into five main headings; reading, writing, listening, talking and feeling, and analyse each of these issues in turn.

Within the 'writing' chapters, we'll be discussing issues like use of plain language, and how to persuade others to our point of view across a range of channels, including email, text and Internet.

Then we'll look at 'talking and listening', where we'll cover the interactive face-to-face elements of communication that are such a big part of our working lives; so we will look at meetings and presentations, and examine some of the current hardware which is commonly used, and misused, like voicemail and Power-Point. And we'll also consider the non-verbal methods of communication that can signal so much, even on a subconscious level.

By way of introduction to these topics, some short notes about the common tools of communication are set out below as a starting point to the more detailed analysis which will follow.

'How to...' – Where to start?

We are continually forming relationships in business. Some are destined to be one-off events, appropriate to a single transfer of information; others are the start of something more significant. What they all have in common is the need to get things off on the right foot, and that is what this section is about. Making the right first impression is simply a case of having a little forethought.

Telephoning

When you are about to call someone up for the first time, avoid the urge to be impulsive; don't just snatch the receiver and dial the number. A bit of pre-planning will do wonders for your 'first impression', making you sound self-assured and businesslike.

Think first of all, about the *purpose* of the call. Often there is some kind of selling to be done, perhaps not in the traditional transactional sense, but to do with an idea, some attempt at persuasion may be needed. Perhaps you would like them to attend a meeting or presentation, or you may need their input and advice on a project you're handling, that sort of thing.

The last thing that people want to hear is a lot of waffle, so jot down on a post-it note the purpose of your call, why it is you've chosen that person in particular to speak to and any reasons that might motivate them to help you.

The two contrasting examples below are similar to real life conversations we have witnessed (the names have been changed)

1. The ad hoc approach. This is how it is often done.

'Hello, can I speak to Benjamin Allen please?'
'Speaking'
'Hello Benjamin, my name's Sue Smith and I work at Hayes Autos, I don't know if this is your sort of thing or not, but they've asked me to ask you, so that's why I'm ringing. I don't know if you know Geoff Oxton, he didn't tell me if he knew you personally or if he'd just seen you speaking at a conference or something. Anyway he saw you last week when you were doing that thing about ethics in your organisation at the Business Breakfast meeting in town, which is something we've been talking about for ages because our customers seem to be more conscious of it these days. So, would you consider, that's to say have you ever done this sort of thing for other companies rather than as just a speech, like on a consultancy basis, not that we could pay much, but just as an advisor for an hour or two'.

2. The planned approach. This is how it should be done.

'Hello can I speak to Benjamin Allen please?'
'Speaking'
'Benjamin, I'm calling from Hayes Autos. My colleague Geoff Oxton saw you speak on ethical trading at the Business Breakfast in town last week, and thought you may be able to advise us on how to put a policy in place here. Is that something you think you could help with?'

The second example is businesslike, to the point, but friendly and open, which contrasts sharply with the unfocussed nonsense of the first.

Face-to-face meetings

As with phone conversations, plan your approach. Think about what the meeting is for and who's going to be there, then in your mind, fast-forward to after the meeting and think what you would like the other parties to be saying about you.

Were you self-assured or cocky?

Did you come across as thoughtful or lacking in any opinion?

Did you contribute useful information or trivia?

As you can see, for every positive outcome there is the risk of a negative. How assertive or quiet or informative you attempt to be will be a matter of judgment on the day. If there is someone else at the meeting who's determined to hog the limelight, it may be better to back off and wait for the opportunity to state your case in a quiet, controlled and measured way, as this story illustrates.

Brad

'At 23 I was the youngest and most successful member of our sales team. I worked for a leading pharmaceuticals company in Massachusetts and boy was it competitive. In those days if I went to a meeting, everyone knew my opinion first, I was no shrinking violet. Twenty years on and I've matured some. Now I'm much more likely to sit back and hear what other folks have to say before offering my opinion. Listening has made me a better manager, a bit more likeable too!'

To help you read these individual situations, the non-verbal communication section later on should prove useful, giving you insight into who is thinking what and where the real power lies.

For the time being here's an example of how you can prepare yourself for meetings, even if you've had little input over the parties involved and the agenda.

An important meeting

To help you develop a greater presence in any given situation, you can conduct a 'merit analysis' to raise your awareness of where you stand. This is nothing more complicated than listing your pluses and minuses when faced with this particular scenario.

'Merit analysis' case study

Nancy is a 28-year-old marketing assistant based in a regional office of a large stationery wholesaler. She has a meeting scheduled with the newly appointed Marketing Director from London, who is touring the regions getting to know the team. There are already signs that a plan is afoot to centralise all the marketing activity in London, something Nancy doesn't want to be a part of. No agenda has been set for the meeting.

This is Nancy's Merit Analysis.

Positives

opportunity to set tone and agenda for meeting (build in contingencies according to how it develops – possible tour of plant, possible visit to top customer)

opportunity to discuss my past experience – draw up thumbnail resume and practise delivery

good knowledge of local marketplace

good cost-tracking in place

evidence of regional initiatives helping win local customer loyalty and new business

common ground – new marketing director used to work in food retailing – so did I (chance to build early rapport)

Negatives

lack of control of budgets (set centrally already)

we don't get to see the big picture

risk of presenting the company in a different way to the other regions

reduction in regional headcount may bring costs down (could be countered by the need to employ more people in London so costs might in fact rise)

communication issues with head office (what can we do to solve?)

You can see that as soon as Nancy starts to list the good and bad things about the situation she faces, a plan begins to form by itself. This isn't a long-winded exercise, it should only take about 15 minutes and just a short amount of pre-preparation time will make a massive difference to your competence in meetings.

Don't make a meal of this kind of planning, but do set 'quiet time' aside well enough in advance to prepare the way. In Nancy's example she has to contact the operations manager to help clear the way for the tour and put a call in to the customer. Your own planning will indicate what else needs to be done in advance of your meeting.

Action

Your one-to-one meeting is about to start, you've taken appearance and presence into account, you should be in a well-prepared state, confident of your ground, with some contingency planning to further bolster your position.

The final element is *action,* the things you do and say during the meeting. As communication is a two way process, your actions will to a great extent be governed by how the other party behaves. In our example above, Nancy is meeting her manager for the first time, with experience we can improve our ability to assess the best way to handle different types of character. Maturity and experience helps us to read people.

Letter, email or other written method

There are special circumstances you have to consider when sending a written piece of communication to someone you don't know. With the other two cases above (phone and face-to-face), you have some chance of judging how the meeting is going and how well your message is being received by the other party, in short, you can alter course a bit if it looks like it's not finding favour. The benefit you have is instant feedback.

Obviously that's something you can't do if you've written to them, as you're not there when they read it. For this reason we urge greater caution, don't take risks with humour or flippancy, and unless you've got a very good reason not to, keep it short!

It's certainly true that in all the scenarios we've described here, you will rely heavily on experience and having your wits about you. What we have discussed, however, is a number of ways you can prepare yourself mentally in advance of these communications, rather than rushing, relying solely on your natural charm!

CHAPTER 3

All about reading

You may think a chapter about reading is too simplistic; after all it is such an everyday occurrence it's almost like having a section on how to breathe or how to walk. Yet, the importance of knowing what, how and when to read is greater than ever, as it remains one of the primary ways we receive information and form opinions about the world around us and our daily business imperatives. This process of *receiving*, in whatever form, is at least half of the two way communication process.

A bit like travel, reading broadens the mind, opens us up to new ways of thinking and expressing ideas and makes us consider issues from different points of view, this is irrespective of the content. It may result in us becoming quite literally more interesting to other people, as we have an ever-wider portfolio of topics to talk about.

Aside from the sheer pleasure of reading something you enjoy, you can improve your own ability to communicate effectively by making your business reading a conscious action, by being selective about what to read, when to and how to.

What to read

> *'You gotta look at everything you're supposed to read and put it into piles, and say to yourself that this is really important, this isn't so important, and that down there...I'm never going to read that!'*
>
> Professor Cary Cooper

We're not here to extol the virtues of one newspaper over another, or compare and contrast a selection of trade magazines, because what you read is really up to you. However, you may find the following criteria useful in making some conscious decisions.

What do you *need* to know for work?

What is the minimum expectation of knowledge about your job and what extra would be regarded as added value?

Where is your individual balance of interest between home news, national news and international news?

How do you like to spend your free time?

What do your friends talk about?

When do you feel you're excluded from a discussion (because you don't know about the subject)?

Who do you admire and what 'knowledge' do they have that you don't?

When you've answered these questions, you should be able to come to a view of where the 'reading gaps' are. It may be that you want to be more of an authority on some aspect of your work, in which case internal publications, your company intranet, or trade magazines could be the best route.

On the other hand, it could be your general knowledge of the world at large that you want to improve (all of which impacts on our working lives in some fashion), and here, a quality newspaper or credible current affairs website will help.

Consider *how many* aspects of knowledge (BREADTH) you are going to cover and the *amount of detail* (DEPTH) you believe is desirable, this will be the key to governing the way you read.

According to...

Lynn Rutter – Oxfam

'The biggest advice I would give is that the world doesn't operate in a vacuum. When I joined British Telecom many years ago, you thought that all you had to do was understand the world of British Telecom and you'd get on in life.

But the people who were successful were the ones who stuck their head above the parapet and saw a world outside British

Telecom. The ones that had spent 20 or 30 year careers only developing the skills of how to work the British Telecom process, found themselves completely lost when they were made redundant.

So my advice would be to set aside time to keep yourself informed. Information will not be handed to you on a plate, you'll have to go and look for it. So attend meetings and presentations being held about the new product or whatever, even if it's not related to you or your job. Take a broader view of what's going on and actively keep yourself informed. Secondly, look outside your own industry. Don't assume if you work for Nokia, for example, that the only thing you need to keep up with is what's happening in other mobile phone companies. Your best ideas often come from completely different industries that are nothing to do with what you're doing'.

How to read

We don't read everything in the same way. Think for a minute about the impact of an advertising hoarding on your consciousness, versus the level of knowledge you absorb from an official document. It is because the messages are designed with different outcomes in mind that our method of taking them in alters.

Environment is also an important factor here. The advertiser, who is trying to sell you something, knows you will only glance at the poster while travelling along in your car. On the other hand, the official document will cover detailed information that will require your full attention.

We are constantly making these assessments of how important information is, without stopping to think about it. Because we return time and again to the theme of conscious communication, it's worth making some value judgements on how to read the different types of information that come your way.

You will, by this stage of your life, have developed an automatic reading style. People who read slowly tend to take every word individually and marvel at those who can skim swiftly through a passage, yet still retain the same amount of information from it.

It's hard to break away from your natural style, but you should try to adapt the way you read according to the importance of the information being presented, increasing your level of 'absorption' for critical information (e.g. like this week's sales figures), and turning it down for more casual, leisure-based reading.

Try this

Most busy managers increasingly rely for their information on the 'executive summary', a page or two of headlines, presented at the front of a report. During one of your high-attention reading sessions try to distil the contents of the article into half a dozen bullet points, without losing any significant facts.

This is a useful exercise because it not only focusses your mind on what you've read, helping you to remember the really important points, but it also lets you practise writing this kind of summary, which you will find useful the next time you are asked to present your ideas on a particular topic.

In practice we need to increase the number of conscious assessments we make of what to read. Here's a real life example to illustrate the point.

You turn up for an important job interview ten minutes early and the receptionist asks you to take a seat. She has also been told to inform you that part of the interview will involve a discussion of a variety of current affairs topics.

A quality broadsheet newspaper is lying on the table in front of you. In the time allowed you could read the whole of the front page, or the headline and opening paragraph of at least two thirds of the stories in the paper. What would you choose to do?

What you've seen so far in this section may have made you decide to read more, if so you need to think about how you're going to fit it in.

When to read

You need to consider two factors. Firstly, in terms of quantity, how much do you need to read? And secondly, what will you have to do to make enough time. If this all sounds a bit too pro-scriptive then think back to some of your good intentions in the past and ask yourself, what it was that got in the way of fulfilling your ambitions, often it's simply about finding the time in our already full schedules.

You might find planning is easier if you think in terms of two sorts of time-slots for reading, core time and bonus time.

Core time is set in stone, you choose it in advance and have it 'booked out' for whatever you've selected, so you could say, 'I will take one hour every Sunday morning, between 10:30 and 11:30 to read my favourite newspaper'. Having a start and end time will also help you to focus how you read, as we discussed in the previous section.

Bonus time is the precious minutes you find yourself with unexpectedly, on the train, over breakfast, while waiting for a colleague to arrive.

You can apply the same principle to the working week by resolving to set aside 15 minutes core time every morning to catch up with the company news letter or intranet site, or to read a relevant trade magazine.

If you're starting to think that living your life like this would drive you mad, remember this; Firstly, you are doing it for yourself, to increase your knowledge and become better informed, and secondly, this core time/bonus time approach doesn't take up your whole life, you may only allocate a couple of hours a week to this activity (and incidentally it should supplement your existing reading, not replace it). Finally, you should find some way of rewarding yourself for achieving your goal, which will increase your gratification in the experience.

In summary

In this chapter we've acknowledged that reading is a critical element of communication, one of our primary methods of acquiring knowledge. Equally we've recognised the amount of time it takes up and because this is such a finite commodity we need to make choices about what we read. That decision-making process can be helped by asking ourselves a few basic questions about what we're trying to achieve with our reading, is it to become more knowledgeable about a particular topic, to increase the breadth and depth of our conversations or to catch up with what's happening in the world of media and entertainment? No doubt it will be a mixture of these things and more, but by making some conscious decisions about what we read, we stand to gain more from the activity.

Staying on an objective and conscious level you can start to take decisions about how to read different articles. An important report that you need to discuss with colleagues may require concentrated effort including some note taking, as in our executive summary exercise earlier. Alternatively, a look through the entertainment guide to see what this week's movies are or catch up on the odd music review probably only requires a quick skim.

We finished by looking at the whole subject of when to read. This is supplementary reading over and above what you would normally do and it's designed to make you better informed about your own choice of subjects.

We now live in a world that could be described as 'content rich'. Technology is increasing the availability and number of media streams, all of which we can use to absorb information and entertainment. What hasn't changed is our ability to read more than one article at a time.

Try this

Online curiosity

Pre-Internet you had to make a conscious effort to exercise your curiosity; it may have meant a visit to the local library, or a bookshop to purchase a relevant text.

Now you can take ten minutes a day to be better informed about an aspect of general knowledge that you haven't explored.

Begin by making a list of all the things you might have been curious about in a fleeting way over the last few months and track down some information online. Think too about what makes the world go round, explore politics, religion, family values and culture, modern history, art and literature, there's a vast array of subjects that your online search will give you an insight into. Best of all you can consume as much or as little as you want at any one time, saving the sites of interest in your 'favourites'.

According to…

Professor Cary Cooper

'What managers do that is so wrong is to read whatever it is that hits their desk. They pick it up and start doing it.

Very often managers will read an email and deal with it there and then, regardless of its' priority, and some of that is about avoidance.

Sometimes there are certain things that they have to do which they hate, so they'll find any excuse to pick up anything from email rather than have to do what they should be doing'.

To counter what Professor Cooper says, there is a school of thought which says we should do the things we hate most first, getting them out of the way and clearing our minds to concentrate on more important things. Leaving tiresome things undone simply saps our energy.

Choose carefully what you read, and always remember that it should either be a pleasure or have a purpose.

The Elevator Test for Chapter 3

- Reading is critical to our absorption of FACTS to help us form OPINIONS

- We have too much to read, setting priorities is vital

- Think about what you NEED to know and WANT to learn, balance these factors to select what you read

- Always keep your selection criteria in mind, make conscious decisions

- Think of reading as a 'special' activity, set time aside for it

- Apply a level of ATTENTION to your reading that's appropriate to its level of IMPORTANCE

CHAPTER 4

All about writing

'Words are like the loose change in your pocket, it's not how many you have, but their value that counts'

Anon

Well-crafted text is one of the most powerful persuaders in the whole spectrum of business communication and learning the techniques of good writing will turn out to be well worth it.

If you need convincing about the significance of the written word, think about it in the following terms; when you send someone a piece of written communication they will receive two things, firstly, the information in your email or letter, and secondly, a means of making value judgements about you the sender.

It's not just what they read, but what they read *into* it that's important.

We're going to be exploring the different types of written communication that are commonly used, and looking at the similarities and differences between them. We'll examine how to establish your own writing 'personality', plus when and how to adapt your style to fit different circumstances.

Perhaps most important of all, we'll analyse ways of using your writing as a means of persuasion, with particular reference to the skill set employed in the advertising industry.

Establishing your writing personality

You have already had a chance to think about different styles of communication, and uncover what is good and bad about each.

If we take the time to reflect on our own current standard, we are in a position to consider how we may go about making some improvements.

It's not a question of trying to write in someone else's style, you have to be true to yourself (it's difficult to sustain for any length of time anyway). So don't try to undergo a personality make-over, just consider that when it comes to the written word there's quite a lot you can do to improve the way you *appear* to others. The style you adopt is important, and we call this 'establishing your writing personality'.

According to…

Professor Chris Brewster

'I like the idea of a 'writing personality', and I definitely think you can develop an individual style as long as you remember to adapt to your audience. Even though I'm an academic now, I've benefited from being a journalist in the past because it helped me realise how to write in a very understandable way. I've tried to develop a style that's very plain and straightforward, whereas some academics choose to speak in a way that some find difficult to understand'.

Try this

You can become more conscious of the impression you make on people, if you take time to analyse the writing personality of others. Spend an hour in the library and pull out, at random three or four books by authors you don't know. Dip into the middle of each and read a passage, then note down what you think the author is like. Are they male or female, what age group are they in, what is their nationality and background?

Next, write down the reasons why you think this. Is it use of language, the story itself, the tone of the piece? Then turn to the inside cover and read the notes about the author to check how accurate you were.

This is a great way of gaining an understanding of how people read *into* what we've written. Thinking and acting in a certain way consistently can be a helpful, part of establishing this personality. Many famous authors have taken pen names, 'becoming' their alter ego for the time they are writing, some notable ones have written as the opposite sex!

What we say and the way we present our written work, is something that reflects the kind of person we are, and in order to be seen in the best light we need to bring a higher level of consciousness to our written communication.

Look back at the word pool exercise you completed earlier, and think about what people would expect of you. If it showed that you're a 'thoughtful intelligent person', then your written work should reflect that, if you came across as more 'laid back and creative', you need to take a different approach to confirm that signal.

In thinking about your personality you need to get the balance of honesty right. Think of your written communication like an advertisement for you as a person.

Presenting things in their best light has always been an important skill in the world of politics, now often referred to as 'spin', but there's a big difference between this and telling lies. It is a matter of which angle you are viewing things from, as John Akers said earlier.

According to…

Peter Sanguinetti – British Gas

'Spin has become part of our lives, the important thing is to determine whether it is a case of putting the facts across in the best possible manner or deliberately misleading people. The latter is unethical, undesirable, ill advised and likely to lead to you being caught out and losing credibility'.

We can all recall incidences in the political arena in recent years where public figures have fallen victim to their own earlier spin, the lesson is, 'handle with care'.

Applying your writing personality

Knowing *who* you are is important, but you also have to be conscious of *how* you present yourself. Many people fall into the trap of trying too hard, particularly if the circumstances of the communication are more formal.

These days, we no longer have to impress other people with our command of big words or flowery language. Plain English is here to stay.

The benefits of simplicity

Look at the following example, which illustrates why Plain English is so important.

In real life conversations no one uses words like 'herewith' or 'perusal', and yet they turn up in job application letters with alarming regularity. Instead of 'please find enclosed herewith my curriculum vitae for your perusal' try, 'I have included a copy of my career history for you to look at'.

Now, if you can't use Plain English well, you are likely to be judged as pompous and condescending. Even in the legal profession, well known for its use of elaborate language, things are changing.

David Harper is Head of the Employment Department at the leading law firm Lovells, and he believes the use of 'legalese' (the old fashioned language that some lawyers still use) is outdated. He has harsh words for those who still persist, and cites three key reasons why they might continue to do so.

Insecurity – if you really did know what you were talking about then you'd put it in simple terms rather than dressing it up to try and confuse your audience.

Arrogance – the belief that these issues are so complex and difficult for the layman to understand, that they need their own specialist form of flowery language to describe them. This is usually misguided.

Uncertainty – a lack of clarity of thinking which results in using a very verbose style to try to mask the fact that you're not sure what you're talking about!

David Harper tells it like it is, and advocates a much simpler, down-to-earth approach to communication. Incidentally, Lovells have won a Plain English award.

The basics of Plain English

The following hints and tips are designed to help you to write better Plain English. They can, and should, be used across all written media. Note also that these rules apply irrespective of your audience. Although it may be tempting to use longer words and more complicated phrases when you are writing to the boss (in an attempt to impress him/her), resist this impulse. They'll see the difference between your speech patterns and your writing, and wonder why you write in this way.

First things first, whatever you're writing, you'll need to start with some form of heading or headline. Even email allows you to do this, so make sure you always fill in the subject field. Stop and think what this achieves. If well written, your headline will grab the reader's attention and draw them into the body of the piece. You can adopt an approach that is either **factual** or **curious**.

A **factual** heading is simply designed to be the shortest form of words you can find to sum up what the body text says. Email is a great discipline for practising this, as when it arrives in the recipient's inbox they will only be able to read the first half a dozen words or so within the subject field. This forces you to be extremely succinct, as in the next example.

A Good Story

Less is more

There are times when fewer words have significantly more power than many. This was certainly the case for one philosophy student who sat in an examination room with his fellow students. The question on the paper in front of them was 'What is a risk?'

While the rest of the students chewed their pencils, furrowed their brows and scribbled furiously, he calmly wrote his answer, stood up and walked out.

The curious adjudicator came to collect his paper.

On it was his two-word answer.

'This is'

Curious headings include questions, puns or puzzles, and they have the same objective of enticing the reader to want to know more. When executed well, this type of opening is extremely effective, but make sure you deliver on your promises. That old trick of putting a headline like 'Free Beer!', and then going on to say 'Now that we've got your attention etc. etc.' is old hat and will simply annoy readers. This is the downfall of much of the 'spam' email we receive. We're now so used to the kind of attention grabbing puff that accompanies this unwelcome intrusion into our inbox, that most of us have given up opening the email itself, knowing that the 'promise' won't be fulfilled. If we do end up being 'tricked', it usually annoys us sufficiently to immediately delete the email, making the attention grabber redundant, along with the rest of the content.

A Good Story

A phenomenon which swept the internet was known as 'Rickrolling'. The idea was to get web users to click on a link by enticing them in with some promise or other, whereupon they would be re-directed to a video of pop star Rick Astley, singing his hit, 'Never gonna give you up'. No doubt Mr. Astley was delighted with the exposure and similar harmless scams are bound to continue.

The point is, this was a joke to fool your friends with, not a serious piece of communication, designed to increase interest in the artistes music!

How to write a good story

The BBC trains its journalists to shy away from putting too much detail in a headline. They recommend that the essence of the story should be summed up in four or five words, and on no account should it stretch over more than two lines.

Their golden rules are as follows:

Sell the story (but don't oversell it, as this can lead to disappointment)

Avoid jargon and clichés (using words like 'slammed' or 'blasted')

Avoid being too cryptic (and remember that all audiences won't be on the same wavelength)

Apart from having a beginning, middle and end, a good story relies on the application of 'some basic rules'.

Editing – tautology is the practice of saying the same thing twice, using different words, and it's a waste of time for both the author and the reader. Avoid repetition, and use clean and efficient phrases to get your message across. When you've finished composing your piece, read it back and delete any unnecessary words. At the same time, you need to try and make sure you maintain the flow of the message. Busy people will soon come to appreciate that you are an effective communicator if you show this clarity of thought through your writing.

Sequence – each paragraph should deal with a single theme. That is to say, it should start out with the core idea, be developed with a sentence or two and, towards the end, signal the expected subject matter of the next paragraph. Writing in this way allows you to order your individual paragraphs into a coherent story that flows in a logical sequence.

A further tip on structure is that you should consider the use of bullets and numbering. This kind of writing has become particularly important for web pages, as Internet users rarely have the time and patience to plough through large blocks of text.

(There is a more detailed section on how to write for the Internet later on). Even a lengthy email can be improved by having an opening section which outlines what is to come in bullet point form. It's a bit like the executive summary we mentioned earlier.

Style – 'Active' is much better than 'passive'. What this means is that you should try to write in a way that puts the 'actor' before the action. Here's an example:

'The president has called for tough action on street crime'.

A passive way of saying the same thing would be as follows:

'Tough action is required on street crime, according to the President'.

Active writing is much more dynamic and engaging for your audience.

Finally, when it comes to style, try to keep your sentences short. This allows the reader a much better chance to pick up the relevant facts quickly and easily.

It's not only in journalism that Plain English is important, all aspects of business benefit if we take the time and effort to simplify what we are saying. Read below the example of how the BBC started an initiative to dispense with waffle.

For some people using Plain English doesn't come naturally, they may believe in the benefits of it, but it just doesn't seem to happen. Here's an example from a business leader who got it wrong.

'I think that a lot of the language of banking and financial services was very opaque, indigestible and inaccessible to ordinary people, and there's been a huge drive to increase the simplicity and the transparency of it'.

It's just a very wordy way of talking about making things plainer, which is all the more ironic in light of the banking crisis, perhaps a bit more plain speaking at an earlier stage may have avoided the situation we all found ourselves in.

The Expert Panel

Russell Grossman

BBC

'The cut-the-crap card was something we introduced in February 2002. Greg Dyke, (former Director General of the BBC) is a football aficionado, so we came up with the idea of a yellow card, like a referee would have and put on it "cut the crap, make it happen".

When we explained it to managers Greg whipped it out and he said, I've had these special cut-the-crap cards made and anybody that wants one can have one. So, if you're in a meeting and you feel that creativity is being stifled then just wave this card.

The device worked partly by using the word "crap" which made people sit up and take notice – The Independent Newspaper reported that it was the 27th most offensive word in the English language – and it sent out the signal that we want to talk in plain English.

So don't send a memo that says "we will commence operations tomorrow", say "we're going to begin work", don't talk about "implementing" a project, talk about "doing" it, don't talk about "procuring" something, talk about "flipping well buying it!"

Using the behavioural example of the cut-the-crap card we've found that people in the BBC both speak and write in a much more direct informal, say-what-you-mean manner and as a result we have less frustration and more general understanding of what people are saying'.

The context of the written word

When it comes to what is acceptable in a written format things change over time, so it's no real surprise when older colleagues start to lament the downfall of good grammar and mourn the passing of a generation who knew when to use a colon versus a semi-colon.

Our view is that writing should be thought of in the same way as design or fashion, it's a thing of its time and it adapts to society's collective changes in attitude.

The introduction of email has had a big impact here. No one sat down and wrote the rulebook for email, and so it has evolved as a unique form of written communication, which is halfway between a letter and a chat on the phone.

Text messaging too altered the landscape, especially in its early form, where it could only be achieved by multiple key presses to select each letter (predictive text came later, followed by full QWERTY keyboards). Twitter and other similar sites have changed the landscape yet again. They have enforced brevity built into them, with a limit of 140 characters per message. It is interesting to note, as the number of communication channels has opened up, the length of messages has gone down.

A further fascinating outcome of all this is that written communication in all forms has become more informal and less bound by rules and regulations. With so many changes around, both technological and sociological, you might start to believe that anything goes, but it doesn't.

The basic rules of written English

Presentation

Just a generation ago the only people in the office who could properly present a piece of written work were the secretaries, now everyone can do it, thanks to well thought-out, user-friendly word processing packages. The down side of this is that most people are self-taught when it comes to layout and presentation, with the result that you tend to see the full spectrum of styles, from the minimalist to the garish!

Many large organisations issue style guidelines, especially if the company's logo is to be incorporated into a document, and you may even find that there are recommended fonts and point sizes to be used on outgoing mail. It is certainly worth checking. It is easy to see this as petty internal policy, but large organisations in particular like to present a consistent face to the world, in all aspects of their communication. It is seen as a central plank of their marketing effort.

If no such guidance is available, here are a few tips to help you get the basics right.

You may think that the more ornate your document, the more likely it is to be read. In most cases the reverse applies. You don't want to distract the reader from the sparkling prose you've put together, and they are unlikely to see fancy presentation as a substitute for worthwhile content. Say what you mean in a plain and simple way, and let your presentation style reflect this, rather than get in the way.

Think 'consistency' all the time. Changes in the size and type of font look sloppy and untidy; it will probably result in the reader thinking you simply couldn't be bothered to check it before it was sent.

Keep your formatting simple; where you have chosen to use bold, italic, or underline etc. make sure there is a good reason, like the signalling of a new subsection by an emboldened sub-heading. This will help to signpost the reader through your document and make it easier to understand and digest.

Use short sentences. We have said this before, but it bears repetition. If you take a leaf out of the advertising copy-writers book, you'll soon see how you can get points across more effectively by keeping your statements succinct. Contrary to popular belief this doesn't make you appear any less intelligent than more wordy colleagues, in fact the opposite often applies.

White space is the report-readers dream. Most people when faced with huge blocks of solid text turn off immediately. Make sure you break up your document with plenty of gaps between paragraphs. Lists of bullet points or diagrams and tables are equally useful in providing some light and shade.

To practise what we preach, here's a list of bullet points summarising our recommended presentation tips:

- Don't get fancy
- Consistency, consistency, consistency
- Keep it simple
- Short sentences
- Use white space

Structure

The specific structure of your written work will depend on its primary aim; a report is rather different to an email. All the same there are some things you need to consider across the spectrum of your work, all of which are designed to make it easier for the reader and therefore more likely they will take notice of what you're saying.

Before the reader gets into the main body of the piece, it will help greatly to manage their expectation early on.

So, you might say the following:

'In 3 sections, this report outlines our current appraisal policy, the results of a recent staff survey on the issue and recommendations for change'.

Or when a call to action is required, you might be more direct, as in this example:

'I'm sending you this email to get your input before Friday's meeting'.

In both cases the reader knows right from the start what to expect.

Usually you need to get the important information across first, so if you were writing a report, this might be in the form of an executive summary at the beginning. In more informal communication, like email, we have alluded to the use of a bullet point summary near the start or alternatively, you can develop a 'set-up' paragraph which in short form outlines the main issues you ideas you intend to cover.

To finish, you should construct a succinct conclusion which summarises the main points of the correspondence and the expected action.

Now you've established a working structure for the document, you need to go back to the start and ensure it follows a logical sequence. Ask yourself the question why each section follows the other and check to make sure you haven't included any superfluous information. Remember, further background reading can always be placed after the main body in an appendix. The reader can then choose to delve deeper if they wish to.

Tone of voice

You may think it's unusual to talk about the written word in terms of 'tone of voice', but it is immensely important as a tool for bringing your writing to life. In the light of what we've seen earlier about the relationships we form through our communication, it's more important than ever that we pay attention to this kind of detail.

As you type onto your computer screen, there is a 'voice' in your head, and the same applies when the document is read at the other end. It's a bit like those old movies where one character is reading a letter they've received, and you hear the voice of the character who sent it.

When your message is read at the other end, you want it to accurately reflect how you were feeling when you wrote it. Contrast the different tones you would expect in some of these examples:

A thank you note to your staff should convey genuine gratitude.

A letter of complaint to a supplier needs to reflect the seriousness of the issue.

Requesting the opportunity to tender/pitch for a piece of business has to suggest legitimate professional interest.

A rallying call to your team should sound genuinely enthusiastic.

We have cited the 'breakdown in communication' as the universal excuse for anything going wrong in the workplace, and this is why tone of voice is important. It is not only necessary to concentrate on what has been said, but also *the way* it has been delivered. Common mistakes are using upper case in email or text (it looks like you're shouting), or very short staccato sentences which can appear curt and rude.

It is much easier to overcome these misinterpretations with a close team who know you, they will simply accept your natural style and not read any ill intent into it, but it does signal how careful we have to be when establishing new relationships, so people don't get the wrong idea. If necessary, get a trusted colleague to proof read important emails or documents before they go out.

The stage of a relationship will often affect the tone we use. In business, it is wise to let your customers dictate this, otherwise too much familiarity and informality at an early stage may begin to look like complacency, or even worse rudeness.

Spelling and grammar

If attitudes really are more relaxed than they used to be you could be fooled into believing you don't need to pay too much attention to spelling and grammar. But think back to what we said earlier about how the recipient of your message will interpret it; not only are they forming a judgment about the communication itself, but also of the sender.

Spell check software is now universally available, so when a document arrives with errors in it, even if it's only an email, it doesn't tell the reader that you're stupid or didn't pay attention in English lessons at school, it sends the signal that *they're* not important enough for you to have read it through before sending it.

According to…

Kay Winsper – Microsoft

'If I receive something with a spelling mistake in, what do you think I concentrate on within that piece of communication? All the messaging is taken away by you being drawn to the things that are wrong, so I think it's imperative to spell check, otherwise it just looks like you don't care, it looks sloppy'.

Although spell check is a great invention, it only 'reads' what you've written; it can't read your mind. This means that words you misspell, which actually make other proper words will not show up – to illustrate the point have a look at the following anecdote, told by a senior executive at a conference.

A Good Story

Always check your smelling

'I fully understand my reputation as a technophobe, but you will all be pleased to know I have recently attended an email training course and have become fully conversant with all the functions available. May I offer you a word of caution however, when using the spell check facility?

Last week I wrote to my head of finance expressing grave concern that we had a considerable 'under spend' against a number of budget lines, as we approached year-end. In a rush, I quickly spell-checked the email and hit the send button.

She replied asking if I really meant what I'd said and when I re-read the document I discovered to my horror that I had written the following…

Dear Dawn,

Please can you contact me urgently to arrange a meeting? It has come to my attention that I have a number of large underpants, which could land us both in deep trouble…'

It may be a witty, even fictitious anecdote, but it does illustrate an important point.

As far as the subject of grammar is concerned, you are better off relying on care and attention than the grammar-check on your computer. The reason for this is grammar is much more subjective than spelling, and although there are some hard and fast rules, there is often room for interpretation too.

Having the computer make suggestions for everything you write, can change the sense that you were trying to convey. It's not that you shouldn't refer to the advice, but don't feel duty bound to always take it. Again, it can be worth checking with a colleague if you are in doubt.

If you are committed to improving your writing style, there are lots of courses available at local colleges that will help, not just grammatically, but with creative input too. Alternatively if you're part of a mentoring scheme set up by your employer, it is an objective you could add to the mix.

How does it sound?

The Carpenter's rule

Time-served craftsmen in any trade are hard to find, and the old school tended to learn their skill in a painstaking way.

Apart from the practicalities, this was often accompanied by short phrases and sayings to remind the apprentice of the golden rules.

Jacko, a carpenter from the old school shared this piece of wisdom with us, 'measure twice, cut once'. It simply means you should check and double check the length of timber you want, before committing the saw to the wood, as once you've done so there's no going back.

Apply the same double check rule to every piece of written work you intend to send out and you will see an instant improvement. More importantly, so will the people you write to.

Reading your written work back twice, gives you the opportunity to look for spelling and grammar errors, but has the extra benefit of making sure that what you're saying *sounds* right. Is it in a logical order, well reasoned, clear and easy to understand? Will the recipient know right away what you are trying to communicate? Is the tone of it what you intended, have you left any room for ambiguity in the way the text is interpreted?

Here are a couple of extra tips for really important written communications. Firstly, if you are not convinced it sounds right then try reading it aloud. If it sounds daft, it probably is. Secondly, if you want to get a much more objective perspective then print out what you've written and check the hard copy. Very often you'll find you see things differently on paper than on screen.

One final check, does what you've written look polite? Have you treated the other party with a degree of respect?

That completes our list of dos, there are some 'nevers' to take note of too:

Never be afraid to use a dictionary or thesaurus (there are some great versions online for quick reference, but having a hard copy to hand is a good thing too)

Never send any written communication without reading it to yourself at least once

Never spell the name of the recipient wrong

Never fail to check your spelling – before computers were invented, misspelled words were a sign of poor education, now with the availability of spell-checkers, they're a sign that you don't care!

Never abandon your natural style and try to look overly clever, if you are clever it will show anyway

Never waffle

Never forget who you are sending this to and why

Never allow ambiguity to creep in

According to…

Jan Shawe – Sainsbury's

'Call me old fashioned but I think good grammar is important. I think particularly these days when a lot of senior people are doing their own emails, and they probably weren't trained as shorthand typists there's the chance that they won't type as well as a trained typist.

However I think that we judge people by their professionalism, so I think a well written note or letter will often show a very good mind, and also there'll be a clarity of message when it's been well crafted which is really important. So I think a well thought through memo is really important, but if it's sloppily written, in terms of not having a beginning a middle and an end, I just think you receive it and you think what jerk wrote this?'

What Jan Shawe says about us being self-taught is true, and it is testament to our inventiveness that people will find their own ways around a keyboard in a style which suits them. The common mistake made by most of us is we don't take enough time to find out how the word processing package really works. You can save yourself hours of time, if you brush up on the tips in tutorial packages, using key strokes instead of the mouse and finding short cuts to commonly utilised actions. Again, the local college or library is a good starting point if you want to hone your word processing skills, many courses are free and flexible, so you can fit them in to suit your other commitments.

Summary

So, we've looked in this chapter at the issue of establishing a 'writing personality', through raising our level of consciousness about who we are. Make your written words match your spoken voice wherever possible. This is most likely to preserve your credibility as people get to know you through a variety of communication channels.

When all else fails be sure to rely on the principles of Plain English, if people can't understand what you're saying, they're unlikely to form a very positive opinion about you. Use the 'carpenter's rule' as a way of sense checking what you've written, and make sure at the same time your spelling and grammar are accurate. Finally, pay attention to who you are writing for and adapt your tone of voice to match the circumstances they'll read it in.

Try this

Write a letter to a friend.

We have not included advice on letter-writing in this text, as so few formal letters are now sent, and there are plenty of guides both on and off line which will give you templates for your layout.

But letter-writing is a great way to practise articulating your ideas, and it gives you a chance to think about grammar, punctuation, plain language and, most importantly, storytelling. You will also be astounded by the reaction you get from your friend, as these days so few of us receive any personal letters.

The Elevator Test for Chapter 4

- Written communication tells the reader something about you as a person, as well as the information it imparts

- Think about how you'd like others to see you, it'll guide your writing personality

- Headlines should be FACTUAL or CURIOUS, either way they must be RELEVANT to the main body of text

- An active style of writing is more engaging than a passive one, put the actor before the action

- Plain English is a critical element of written communication

- Short sentences, white space and simple phrasing produce a format that's easy to read

- Spelling and grammar are important!

- Apply the carpenter's rule and check (read through), everything twice before you commit yourself

CHAPTER 5

Persuasion

The power of the pen

How much of your communication involves persuasion? The answer is, probably most of it. You don't just find it at the sharp end of business, the sales presentation or the selection interview, it's happening all the time in meetings, emails and phone calls, we are forever trying to get other people to see things our way.

It's such a critical element of communication in today's workplace that we've set aside an entire chapter to analyse it and outline how it can be done better. Much of this is achieved by reference to the advertising industry, where persuasion is the daily bread and have taken our inspiration from the things copywriters do to get our attention and then our money.

Why is advertising so important in the way we communicate?

You might find this form of communication the most irritating of all, clogging up your daily paper, cluttering your browsing, invading your radio listening, upsetting the continuity of your TV viewing, but advertising can teach us a huge amount about how to get our message across effectively. It is their business.

According to…

Alistair Smith – Alite

'I think that advertising has got a great deal to teach communicators and public speakers in a range of different ways because it communicates the key message creatively and through all sorts of disturbing questions, which can arise as a result of telling a story.

It can also pose a problem or engage your attention in subtle or very direct ways but it's fronting the message all the time and asking you to pay attention. So as a professional communicator it's telling you not to lose sight of the end user and to convey your message in ways that they can make sense of and transfer to their own lives'.

Understanding some key principles will help to achieve the following:

Cut through information overload – your 'audience' is being fed more and more messages every day, though a seemingly endless array of new devices, how then can you make sure they take notice of what you have to say? What can you do to make them notice you?

Hard-hitting key messages – if you can find a way of stripping your communication down to its bare essentials and discover techniques that will emphasise the key issues you are more likely to be effective.

The art of persuasion – answering the question, why should people see things your way? What arguments can you put up to convince others to your point of view? How do you go about constructing that rationale?

Accurately interpret the messages you receive – knowledge of the techniques used in advertising should help you understand the communications in your inbox. You'll be better able to see the truth beyond the spin, all of which helps when you're crafting a reply.

What makes advertising work?

> *'Only half of advertising works, the trick is knowing which half'*
>
> Henry Ford

From this you will gather that it's not an exact science, if it were, a lot of advertising executives would be out of work, because we'd all be able to do what they do. Experience can teach us about things like the timing of the message, the audience it's aimed at and the content of the advertisement, but there are other aspects that are much harder to pin down, like the human psyche and how the brain processes data and information.

We start by looking at what is currently known about the principles of effective advertising, once we've got an understanding of that we can think about how it applies to our own everyday communication.

It all begins with who we are talking to.

Target audience

One of the most important lessons we can learn from the world of advertising, is the significance of the target audience for any piece of communication.

It is one of the fundamental rules that we must keep the reader in mind throughout the process.

According to...

Russell Grossman – BBC

'You have to remember in most organisations the audience is so diverse that there can be no single model of communication, so the way you communicate has to be adaptable'.

For now though, consider how the type of person you are writing for, might influence the way you put your message across. It is only when you have some empathy with the recipient that you can begin to understand how they will consume what you have sent.

How would you react to the two different scenarios below?

1. Your mother is retired and sees you roughly one weekend in four as she lives some distance away. You decide you'll keep in touch more regularly by writing letters to her.

2. Your boss has to go to a meeting in an hour's time to justify this month's sales figures, which are 10% below target. She has asked you to email her with the reasons you believe this has happened.

Of course the content of the two pieces of correspondence will differ hugely, but you also need to take account of the circumstances of the person reading your message, this is why we have chosen such diverse examples, to help illustrate the point.

In the first scenario the reader has time on her hands and is interested in the detail, even the trivia, of your existence. In the second example there is an urgency that demands succinct, accurate information that can easily be interpreted and digested, it is all a bit 'no-frills'.

Sometimes you are trying to get a message across to a range of audiences at the same time and this is when life gets difficult. Keith Harris has extensive experience of the finance industry and was Chairman of the English Football League in August 2000.

The Expert Panel

Keith Harris
Seymour Pierce

When I worked in finance, the audience I was communicating with was broadly within a range of quite narrow parameters. However, the population of people you're communicating with in football is very diverse and the parameters very wide. Not only is the breadth huge, but within it, the mix is unbelievably different and that's whether you're dealing with the public at large or the chairmen or with regulators, it's very, very tough.

It's made even more difficult because the needs of the fans aren't the same as the needs of the Chairmen, and you also have to realise that the management of the clubs, both commercially and financially, is very poor.

So communication is made more difficult by a wide range of stakeholders, each with different interests, compounded by an industry where clear-thinking is a rarity. We sought further corroboration of this from the former Managing Director of Arsenal Football Club, Keith Edelman whose background was in retailing as Chief Executive of Storehouse PLC.

Football is a unique example which outlines some of the complexities of communicating with a range of interested parties, but the matrix of target audiences in many businesses is just as intricate, and it takes skill and experience to navigate through.

The Expert Panel

Keith Edelman
Arsenal F. C.

I think retailing and football are similar in that they both deal with the consumer.

The major difference is that in retailing you have to win your consumer from the competition and you have to keep on doing that. In football, you've got to manage your consumer because people don't change teams just because you put your prices up or you're not playing as well, people tend to stay with a club for life.

That leads you to communicate in a different way, it's more friendly, it's more intimate because you are literally all part of the same club in the widest sense.

I think many retail organisations would die to have the kind of relationship with their customers that we have with our fans, but I think that they'd find when they'd got it they might wonder about it.

I'll give an example, if you increase the ticket price here at Arsenal, which you could sell 5 times over, people will write in and say this is a ridiculous increase why have you done it, and you explain it involves the economics of the business. They will still renew the season ticket; but the issue is that they want to get something off their chest.

If it happens in retail there's much less intimate a relationship, so if people still want it they'll buy it, but they're unlikely to complain because they know they have free choice in a retail environment to go somewhere else. In a football environment, they don't have free choice.

Making your advertisement work

In an overcrowded and competitive marketplace, three factors need to coincide to maximise your chance of being noticed above the other players. These are the founding principles of all good advertising campaigns.

Reach – how many different people are able to receive your message at any one time?

Frequency – how often will each individual receive your message?

Quality of message – how appealing is it?

Rather than examine these three factors through an analysis of a global multi-media advertising campaign, it is simpler for us to go back to basics and think about a stallholder at the local open-air market. A big booming voice is likely to be an asset, as it carries further reaching a larger number of people.

Stand nearby for a few minutes, and you'll hear the same messages repeated again and again. This has two benefits, firstly, it's a constant reminder of the key things the barker wants you to remember and, secondly, it takes account of the fact that in a bustling marketplace, different people are moving in and out of earshot all the time.

Finally, consider the stallholder who is known as a local character, he/she indulges in endless amusing banter with passers-by. The entertainment value can enhance the buying experience; it may even mean they can charge a premium.

The circus ringmaster and newspaper salesman employ the same skills, and it's only a short leap from there to many of today's commercial radio campaigns. If we think about our own communication in this way, applying the principles of reach, frequency and quality of message, we are much more likely to be able to persuade the audience to our way of thinking.

Creativity

If you've ever been involved in arranging advertising you will know the media base their rates on the size of audience they deliver. Broadcast media tend to evaluate campaigns on the basis of frequency too, as the number of times the consumer sees or hears the commercial, is a key influence on their ability to recall it leading to an increase in sales of the product.

Today's audience measurement software, which is used to assess campaigns is extremely sophisticated. It is, if you like, the *science* of advertising and a vital part of planning, if the budget is to be spent wisely. The *art* comes into the final of our three elements, that of 'quality of message'.

There seems to be no way of accurately assessing what will capture the public's imagination, no magic formula that can be applied to any product to make it stand out from the crowd. Really great advertisements though are likely to be one or more of the following:

Spectacular
Interesting
Fashionable
New
Different
Funny

The best advertising uses a combination of factors. The final one in the list, 'humour', is a fantastic way of engaging an audience, but it's risky too, as it doesn't always go according to plan.

A Good Story

Cinzano Bianco

The 1970s saw a boom in the sales of Vermouth, with the Cinzano and Martini brands battling it out, head-to-head. A series of classic commercials was produced using popular comic actor Leonard Rossiter and iconic English actress Joan Collins, well known for character roles that were sophisticated and self-assured. Each in the series of commercials built on the last, the running gag being that Collins always ended up having the glass of Cinzano spilt down the front of her expensive dress.

In spite of the amount of attention the campaign attracted, it resulted in increasing the sales of the rival Martini product, for the simple reason that too much of the focus was on the humour and too little on the brand itself.

This salutary tale is worth keeping in mind when contemplating the use of humour in your own written work. To be effective, it needs to be in harmony with the message, to complement it in some way, otherwise the joke will overshadow the point you are attempting to make.

How to write great copy

There is a massive benefit in being able to write great advertising copy, as so many of the lessons can be applied elsewhere in your communication. You should find these techniques can be applied to other forms of writing too.

Case study

The company car

Let's say you need to get support for a project you're working on, appeal for a greater allocation of resources, or put together a compelling argument for why you should have a company car, whatever it is you can use the knowledge of how advertising works to add weight to the case.

Taking a brief

We start with the first step, taking the brief. In the real world of advertising this process can take a lot of time and effort but without it you have no starting point for your writing. Brief-taking can be simplified into an a,b,c process as you'll see below.

a. Who are we talking to?
b. What do we want them to do?
c. Why should they do it?

Before we examine those three simple questions in more detail, there is a golden rule that must always be applied, which is, 'Is 'c', a good enough reason to make 'a' do 'b', if not start again!'

This will be easier to understand in practice, so let's apply the principles to the issue of convincing your boss that you need a company car.

The brief will be answered in the following way:

a. Who are we talking to?
My immediate boss, the budget holder

b. What do we want them to do?
Exercise his/her discretion over the company car budget and provide me with a vehicle

c. Why should they do it?
I already claim mileage allowance when I use my car on company business at a much higher rate than the cost of running a company vehicle.

Each month for the last six my business mileage has increased, as I get more involved with visiting customers.

I am now regularly asked to represent my team at the monthly meeting in Swindon (240 miles round trip).

I understand that there is a shortage of my kind of skills in Swindon and I may at some point be asked to do a day or two a week there.

I am currently considering changing my car as it is old and unreliable; to do this I would need to consider a finance option.

Last month my car broke down on the way to Swindon and I only arrived in time to catch the last five minutes of the meeting.

I have achieved all my objectives for the last two years and would see this as the company recognising and rewarding my efforts.

On days when I am based in our main office, other members of staff could use the vehicle as a pool car.

So now we have answered all three parts of the brief, let us look again at that golden rule.

'Is "c" a good enough reason to make "a" do "b"?, if not, start again!' That is, have we provided a strong enough rationale in answering the third question to make the object of the first question (the target audience), do what we want them to (take the action listed under question b?)

If you had answered question 'c' with 'my friends will be impressed that I'm driving a brand new car', or 'Lynne got a car last month and she's only been here less than a year' you are unlikely to convince 'a' to do 'b'. The reasons have to be focussed on the needs of the audience, not your emotions.

The most important thing you've done here is to present the *business* case to make the decision easy, i.e. providing a car will save the company money in the long run and make you more efficient. You might expect your boss to put your reasons through a rigorous inspection to make sure they stand up, so you may want to provide a more in-depth financial analysis yourself.

Often decisions aren't clear-cut, and you have to try and see what underlies the logic. In this case, your boss will be trying to ensure that this decision is SEEN to be fair on business grounds (so that any hint of favouritism can be dispelled).

Now we've outlined the process, you have a chance to try out a practical exercise which further emphasises the point. Again, we've presented a brief with our three-stage process. This time it's up to you to write the copy (in the form of a letter), in no more than 250 words. You can then compare your version with the one we've written, and make a list of the similarities and differences.

Strictly speaking, there is no right and wrong, but what you will be attempting to do is develop a well-argued case for what you propose; one which covers the main reasons why your audience should do what you ask.

EXERCISE – WRITING BETTER COPY

You work for a company that manufactures nails, and are just about to launch Supa-nail, a revolutionary new product made from hardened steel with a smooth silicon coating that allows the nail to be knocked in quicker.

Your boss has given you the job of inviting your top 50 existing customers to a launch reception aimed at demonstrating the benefits of the new product, with the expectation that orders will follow.

The invitation is to be sent out in the form of a letter.

The brief is as follows

Who are we talking to?
Existing customers who use our nails in a variety of applications.

What do we want them to do?
Attend the launch of Supa-nail so we can show them the benefits of the new product, in the hope that they will spend more with us in future.

c. Why should they do it?
There are strong personal relationships between our company and many of its customers.

This is a chance to see a revolutionary new product and to be an 'early adopter' of it, which will make you appear more dynamic to your own customers.

On the night there will be a prize draw for a 25% discount off your first order.

Because of the way they are made, Supa-nails are faster to use and more reliable – lower failure rates of your end-product help to reduce costs.

You will have a chance to network with potential new partners, as well as rubbing shoulders with your competitors. (SEE NOTE BELOW)

You will get an insight into the advantages of the new product and as such may be able to develop applications that will give you the edge in your own marketplace.

Additional background information

Your company has been facing stiff competition from abroad. Imported nails are cheaper though there is some evidence of higher failure rates as they are made of inferior quality material. Your customer base is loyal in the main, although some now have a mix of suppliers, including the cheaper overseas companies.

NOTE: It's worth putting this in the brief but you may choose to play it down in the final invitation, on the basis that it may put off as many customers as it encourages. They may feel nervous of the competition and protective of their own 'trade-secrets'.

We have compiled a version of the letter, and it is set out below, but resist the temptation to look at it until you've written your own. Let us emphasise, it is only one answer, and any well crafted piece of writing, which adheres the rules we have laid down will be effective.

Dear Mr. So-and-so,

PRODUCT INNOVATION SET TO REVOLUTIONISE OUR INDUSTRY

We would like you to join us for the launch of Supa-nail on Wednesday January 22nd, so you can be one of the first to see this revolutionary new product.

For many years our industry has relied on conventional nails and although adequate for most needs we have become increasingly aware of the problems caused by failure rates. This has been especially true in the economy nail sector, resulting in down time for many of our customers.

In response to this, our innovation team has developed Supanail, combining the toughness of hardened steel with the smooth finish of a silicon coating, for faster insertion into a range of materials.

We would value your company at the launch, when you will be able to do the following:

See Supa-nail in action and try it for yourself

Discuss how Supa-nail can increase productivity in existing applications

Talk to the Supa-nail development team about new applications

Network with industry colleagues

Give yourself competitive advantage when you invest in Supa-nails

In addition to all this we'll be holding a prize draw during the evening where you can WIN A 25% DISCOUNT OFF YOUR FIRST ORDER!

The event will run from 18:30 to 20:00 hours at our Head Office in Slough. We look forward to seeing you.

R.S.V.P.

Yours sincerely

Your own version of the letter will no doubt differ, but check to see if you've covered the main principles. Consider whether you have talked the language of the target audience, have you gone on to tell them what you want them to do? Most importantly of all, have you succinctly outlined the reasons they should do it?

Does the data you've provided them with offer enough of an incentive to attend?

Look again at the letter we've written, and you'll find the following practical and creative elements.

Headline – something to draw the reader in, a summary of what this is all about

Empathy – created by showing understanding of some of the problems that the recipient is facing

Call to action – what do you want them to do?

Summary – bullet points that give all the information quickly and succinctly

Reward – an incentive that answers the question 'what's in it for me?'

Logistics – when, where

How much puff?

It has always been accepted that there will be a degree of licence taken with advertising, showing products and services in their best light to attract the customer. The term for this is 'advertising puff'. Legal precedent in the U.K. was set in this area by a very famous case.

A Good Story

Carlill and Carbolic Smoke Ball Company – all puff and nonsense?
This important case in English law dates back to 1893.

The wonderfully named Carbolic Smoke Ball Company advertised that anyone who bought their product, used it in the directed manner and still caught influenza within a year would receive £100 (a lot of money at the time).

Mrs. Carlill followed the instructions, but still fell ill (what a surprise!). She then wrote to the company, no doubt between her coughs and sneezes, to claim her 'compensation'. The company argued a point of law to do with offer and acceptance, claiming that no reasonable person would consider their advertisement to have been an offer capable of being accepted. In addition they said that their advertisement had not been an offer at all, but was merely promotional 'puff'. The judges disagreed with both of these points and Mrs. Carlill took her place in legal history and, no doubt, her £100 too.

The line between what is and isn't acceptable is thin, but a good guide is that the more specific and exaggerated the claim, the more likely it is to fall foul of the law. Carlsberg, for example, used to be advertised as 'the best lager in the world', but has now been updated to remain lawful to 'probably the best lager in the world'.

How advertising has changed the way we communicate

The relevance of all this to our daily communications is that it makes us more inclined to take things with a pinch of salt, we're far more likely to ask, 'what's the catch?' In turn, this makes it more and more difficult to make an impact when we're asking other people to believe our claims. Perhaps this is why Ronseal, the manufacturer of wood stains and varnishes began to use the line, 'it does exactly what it says on the tin'. Advertising is constantly seeking to re-invent itself, and this back to basics approach has become a national catchphrase.

Under these circumstances it's all the more important to stick to the a, b, c rules of answering the brief, whether it's selling the case for more flexible working hours to your team or persuading your peers to share information more readily with the group.

To illustrate this, here's a relevant anecdote.

A Good Story

The best advertisement ever written
Think about all the rules of good advertising, about how you need to target your message as specifically as possible to your

particular audience, hit them with it as often as you can and have the right creative treatment to help them remember it.

The best advertisement ever written in our opinion, was a poster site on a main route into Manchester in the mid nineties. It simply had three massive letters filling the entire space, it said

OTS

This campaign was aimed at media buyers, the people who recommend the most effective kind of advertising for their clients. We talked about 'frequency' earlier, and one of the key methods of assessing the likely success of a campaign is to calculate the number of times your target audience is likely to see the advertisement. In poster advertising this is referred to as OTS, or 'opportunities to see', and the higher the OTS, the greater the predicted success of the campaign.

What this poster said in effect, was 'recommend poster advertising to your clients'. It was superbly targeted, as only those in the know in advertising would understand what OTS stood for, each time they passed it they made a mental note of the opportunities to see and the very fact that they made the connection suggests that the quality of message was superb.

An example of a creative treatment that was supreme in its simplicity. We can pick up a lot of great communication techniques by taking notice of how advertisers try to entice us.

Try this

Watch the TV commercials
Instead of skipping through the ads, make a conscious effort to watch them.

The really essential viewing for the committed communicator is TV advertising. Pro rata it is the most expensive form of television production, even outstripping costume drama on a second for second basis. What that translates to is highly sophisticated messaging, delivered in an alluring (and often hugely expensive), way to a particular group of viewers with a specific desired outcome. Add to this list the fact that mostly the advertiser has only 30 seconds or less to get their message across and you can start to appreciate the skill of the communicators involved.

Of course it's not *all* high art, but with such huge sums of money involved it is often well thought out, brilliantly executed and highly entertaining. Recent times have seen the growth of viral campaigns, clips which become internet hits by word of mouth or via social networks. Sometimes the two media interconnect with people being drawn to watch a TV commercial online because they have heard about it from others. The Cadbury 'gorilla' campaign was one such example.

While you're watching any of this content, try to work out what was in the minds of the creators, who were they aiming this advertisement at and what did they want the target group to feel after they'd seen it. Make a note of your best and worst commercials, and find a mentor, friend or colleague to discuss them with. You can add some value to this exercise by deliberately including examples that are not aimed at you. Look at how some products are aimed at the opposite sex, or take time out to watch a commercial break during teenage TV and see what they are being asked to buy and what methods are used to convince them.

The Elevator Test for Chapter 5

- Advertising can teach us valuable lessons about persuasion, a key element of effective communication

- As well as understanding WHO your audience is, you need to be aware of HOW they will consume your message

- Effective advertising campaigns comprise 3 elements, reach, frequency and quality of message

- Great commercials are memorable through being interesting, new, different or funny

- When making specific claims, don't over exaggerate benefits, you'll only be found out

- Taking time to analyse commercial campaigns gives you insight into the art of persuasion

CHAPTER 6

Writing – the rules of the tools

Email

'I don't want to discourage young people from feeling they can copy me on emails, but I wish people would use it a bit more responsibly'.

Bill Dalton – HSBC

Five years ago, email was the dominant form of written communication in the workplace. It probably still is, in most businesses, but what has changed is the expansion in ways it can be delivered. No more the fixed PC on the desk, we have moved through laptops of varying shapes and sizes onto Blackberry, iPhone and other smartphones, and more recently on tablets like the iPad.

While the number of devices has increased, the integration on any individual one has expanded, so now you can use a phone for text, data, photos, music and more. There is a rumour you can actually call someone from it!

Email's rise to supremacy happened very quickly, it very soon became the most popular form of written communication, firstly, within organisations and then in dealings with suppliers, customers and other stakeholders. One executive illustrated the speed of acceptance of this new delivery channel with the following story.

'When my son reached 4 years of age he went through a phase of asking each evening, "what did you do at work today Daddy?".

One night I had been through the usual round of explanations, delivered in language he'd understand (I spoke to some people on the phone, met up with some of my friends at work to talk over some things etc.), then realised I had no adequate explanation for what I'd spent most of the day doing.

Finally, with a flash of inspiration, I said, "you know Daddy's laptop computer that he works on at home? Well, I wrote some letters on my computer and sent them to other people's computers". Satisfied with this explanation I sat back'.

After a pause, the boy replied, 'Daddy, why didn't you just email them?!'

Sadly, the speed of uptake of email has only been matched by the speed of abuse of it. It seems now most people in business aren't sure whether to treat it as friend or foe. Here are some views from both sides.

Email problems

'Well, if you want my opinion' – this sums up the 'reply-all' syndrome. This can happen when an organisation wants to communicate with all staff at the same time, perhaps over a controversial issue, like cost reduction or a matter of ethics. Having had everyone's email address dumped into the 'To' field, some people simply can't resist the opportunity to let the world know how they feel. So they reply all with their 'I think this is outrageous' stance. Sometimes this escalates into war of words between those in favour and those against an issue, wasting everyone's time.

'Look how hard I work' – technology has allowed an all-hours culture to develop in lots of organisations, as people can log on from home at any time. If you're regularly receiving email from your boss in the small hours of the morning, it won't be long before you feel duty bound to match their diligence. In some organisations, the culture supports this behaviour, and it becomes a badge of honour to be seen to be working into the middle of the night. The truth is, over time a long-working-hours culture is often destined to lead to stress, perhaps resulting in increased absenteeism, so it may end up working against the organisation.

Stonewalling – (a defence mechanism). Considering email is a virtually instantaneous method of communication, it's amazing how it can slow down any process or decision-making. One trick that is often employed is to deliberately misinterpret the question being asked, or to continually ask for further clarification of certain points. There are probably deeper underlying problems behind this behaviour and they need to addressed first, in order to prevent the behaviour escalating.

Too shy for words – email has turned some party animals into shrinking violets as they hide behind their screen, hunched over the keyboard all day. It's not uncommon for people at adjacent desks to email each other rather than engage in that age-old communication method, 'the conversation'. Social interaction is an important part of working life, and can lead to a reduction in stress. Abandoning it could be dangerous.

Spamming the boss (for overload) – when people really don't like their boss they can use email to tie them up in knots. This is especially true if there is collaboration within the team, where they agree between them that they'll all send as much email (relevant or otherwise) to the boss, and where possible call for action to be taken. Even if the only action necessary is a reply, this in itself can use up massive amounts of management time.

'I can't tell you this to your face' – cowards use email to deliver the kind of bad news that should be handled sensitively and on a face-to-face basis. There are reported cases where people have been made redundant via email. Equally the medium is too often used for disciplinary matters (see below).

'I'm so annoyed with you' – handling conflict is an area that lots of us find difficult. Email allows inept managers to shout at colleagues, subordinates, even the boss, without ever having to face down the situation. The copying in of other parties can add to the humiliation of the intended recipient and, worse still, there's a verbatim record of what's been said which may come back to haunt all concerned.

'Now, it's your problem' – some people feel they can dump their workload on to others by email. This is not an effective way of delegating tasks. Being at the receiving end of a list of tasks to complete at the end of a long week can be frustrating, especially when you know the other party is going home to enjoy a guilt-free weekend having cleared their inbox into yours.

Access all areas (getting to the CEO) – Who you can reach used to be limited by your position in the hierarchy, but no more. Now you can get to everyone whenever you want. What might seem relevant to the sender can sometimes be of little relevance or importance to the recipient and if this results in them not replying it leaves staff with the feeling that their views aren't listened to.

According to…

> Bill Dalton – HSBC
>
> 'I'm Chief Exec of HSBC bank plc. This bank's got 50,000 people, and before email, people who work in the bowels of the organisation wouldn't think of sending me a copy of their latest work, but they do now.
>
> Before, to send something on paper to me was a big deal, now it's easy, it might even be cool, but the main reason that people do that is it gives them a chance to put something in front of the Chief Exec that they never had a chance to put in front of them before.
>
> But what most people don't tell you is what really happens to all that email. For example I know other companies where the CEO has said they welcome email from everyone in the organisation and that sounds wonderful, but unfortunately it's only going one way.
>
> They actually have someone in their office looking at those emails and saying "hey, look at what this bozo wants", so I

don't want to do that, I want to be honest with the people who work in this bank'.

<u>'I've got written proof'</u> – ('well I sent you the email, look I can prove it') – of course your sent items box can be a great comfort, if you've forgotten whether or not you've actioned something. Equally it can be turned to bad effect to catch other people out and the fact that all emails are timed and dated gives even more ammunition if your request hasn't been acted upon.

According to...

Bill Dalton – HSBC

'There's an awful lot of upward delegation going on, because if I don't look at a particular email, if I ignore it and there's something in there, that goes badly wrong 6 months from now, the person that sent it to me will say, it was in the email, so that's a problem'.

Many of the negative aspects of email were highlighted during our interviews with experts. Perhaps the most charming were the aesthetic objections from one source.

According to...

Keith Harris – Seymour Pierce

'I'm not a big fan of email, I've always been averse to screens, I've got a beautiful antique desk and I don't want some poxy screen on it'.

Finally, a few experts expressed the following opinion as long as we promised to preserve their anonymity.

'I wish there was a button you could press which sent an automatic reply saying, you're confusing me with someone who gives a damn!'

Anon

Email benefits

Faster than a speeding bullet – the trouble with the conventional postal service is that everything takes so long. Now message sending and receiving is virtually instantaneous. You can be talking to someone on the phone, send them the relevant attachment, and hear the 'ping' of their computer as it arrives. This has speeded up all aspects of business dealings, increased efficiency and facilitated higher productivity.

'Let's be friends' – because of the way email has evolved it tends to be much less formal than other kinds of written communication, and as a consequence much friendlier. Used well it can be a great way of engaging people very quickly. When many businesses are built on relationships, this can help to strengthen the bonds with your customer base, or suppliers.

More than words can say – greater bandwidth has removed the shackles from email. They are no longer restricted to the written word. Increasing amounts of data can be fed down the line, including pictures, video, graphics, presentations and more. This opens up possibilities for all kinds of businesses who used to have to rely on conventional methods of data delivery.

When memory loss is a problem – 'did I call that meeting for 10 or 10:30?' With email you can always check your written record, not only of what you've said to 'them', but what 'they' have said back. Used positively, this written record can be referred to later as an audit trail of who said what. There are also cases when what has been written has been permissible as evidence in tribunals, so we sometimes need to think before we press 'send'.

Fully flexible – now that home working has become commonplace we are no longer tied to the office to finish everything off. Instead, we can return to our families then log on and deal with email in the same way as we would during the working day. Mobile devices have allowed for this facility during commuter time too.

'Hear ye! Hear ye!' – as a form of mass communication email is hard to beat. It happens in real time and, more importantly, it's simultaneous in its delivery. This means that if you have to tell people the same story at the same time, you can deliver the message to everyone's inbox in a single hit.

According to...

Michael Broadbent – HSBC

'HSBC Holdings now employs over 215,000 people world-wide, so email gives you an enormous advantage over the historic tyranny of size and distance, especially when you're spread over 80 countries and territories'.

We have laid out the major arguments for and against email, but ultimately it's about how well it's used that matters. Here's a balanced view from Surinder Hundal HR and Internal Communications Director of Nokia.

The Expert Panel

Surinder Hundal
Nokia

Email makes it much easier to communicate across time zones and across borders, so it removes some of the artificial barriers, it's also very cheap and you can do things very very quickly. On the negative side, there is a tendency to over use email and not only in terms of the *quantity* of messages but also, I would argue, in the *quality* of messages you generate.

By that I mean people tend to become too dependent on conducting their business through email, when it may be better to think about the situation and decide if it could be handled face-to-face or by a phone call. I think we're also beginning to lose that skill of fitting the situation to the medium.

There can be a tendency for people to hide behind their laptops and build relationships with their computers rather than other people, especially if you're not part of a big team. We think that if you're not careful this could start to have an impact on culture, not only in terms of social culture but also in the way we actually solve problems and deal with situations.

The second aspect is one where because you're hiding behind a PC it's easier to send an angry email, it's called 'flaming', and that's something that can get compounded and create a culture that is very direct. On email you don't have any niceties like a conversation about the weather or some other social preamble.

The third aspect is that people use email badly and so you get a message, which has got about 400 pages of previous emails attached all of which just clogs up your system.

To try and get over this at Nokia we have a basic policy of 'netiquette', that lays out some obvious 'do's' and 'don'ts', and periodically we have a burst of noise that reminds people about what is good practice.

It helps to understand the good and bad of email, so we can try to make sure our outgoing messages don't compound the problems associated with it. If you work as part of a small team you can also try to convert your colleagues to this way of thinking which should help to lessen the number and improve the relevance of the messages hitting your inbox.

Beyond this the 'burst of noise', referred to by Surinder Hundal, is a good way of reminding a larger group of people about the best way to use email.

Try this

Learn to touch type.

Like paying into a pension scheme or brushing your teeth, touch-typing is something you should start doing as young as you possibly can. You can probably find lots of reasons why not to bother, for a start it's hard (especially at first), and time consuming, but the results are worth it.

The main benefit is speed, it's not inconceivable that you could double your current typing speed, saving you valuable minutes or even hours each day, which could add up to months or years over the course of your lifetime. A second advantage is that when you have mastered the skill, you can hit the right keys almost unconsciously, leaving your mind free to think about what it is you're writing. In this way, we can concentrate more on the content than where the keys are. There are lots of software packages and instruction books available and by setting aside maybe 15 minutes a day, first or last thing or during your lunch break you'll soon get the hang of it.

One further tip, you don't even have to be that good, unless you aspire to be P.A. to the Managing Director. Spelling and grammar checking will pick up most of your errors and you should always re-read your material before you send it anyway, to see if there's a better way of saying what you've said.

The last word on email comes from Chris Major, Head of PR at AstraZeneca, one of the World's Top five pharmaceutical companies, who sounds a warning to all of us who rely so heavily on email for our business dealings and to share gossip with friends.

'I think that people sometimes naively believe that an email is somehow not a public communication'.

A sobering thought.

Short messaging – texting

> *'Text is so instantaneous, when it goes off I can resist reading it'*
>
> Anon

New technology is never new for very long, but fortunately when it comes to communication, the rules that apply to existing channels and devices can generally be applied to whatever comes along.

The popularity of texting took even mobile phone manufacturers Nokia by surprise, and the uptake has been a modern communications phenomenon. Early adopters of the technology were teenagers, who found that this highly intimate way of keeping in touch not only proved cheaper than standard cellphone calls, but was also considered 'cool' in the early days.

In its early incarnations, text tended to be used in a social context, but increasingly it has become accepted as a business tool. No longer is it the preserve of teenagers, as improvements in the technology have made it accessible in the mainstream. Some commercial organisations were quick to seize on this new way of reaching customers, for others it became a great way of sending diary reminders or updates on projects.

The following pages look at texting as a way of communicating in business, and examine the pros and cons of the technology.

Criteria for texting

When you're thinking about the 'who', 'what', 'where', and 'why' of texting, the most important factor to remember is how intensely personal a device the mobile phone is. Before mobiles were invented, the house or office phone was accepted as a shared piece of equipment used for communication. Now people are far more likely to see their mobile as their individual access to the world on a one-to-one basis.

Stop and consider this before using text as a business tool. At the very least, it is still considered good etiquette to ask permission. Increasingly, we are happy to receive alerts on our mobiles, many use them for aspects of banking, including being given warning when we are about to go overdrawn.

Doctors surgeries and dentists often have inbuilt systems which automatically alert patients of their upcoming appointments, so there are times when texting is not only useful, but desirable by both parties.

The difficulty comes when people feel their personal cyberspace has been invaded by either unsolicited text, or if they have given their number for some spurious reason, only to find it has turned up on a database and is being used by a marketing company.

Even businesses who believe they are providing useful information can get it wrong. A chain of estate agents started texting potential purchasers with details of houses that might suit their needs. Although the recipients understood why the service was being provided, they had not given express permission to the estate agent, and the problem was made worse once a suitable property had been found (often via another agent). Yet the messages continued to come through.

One recipient put how he felt into words like this.

'I knew they were only trying to help and part of me thought it was okay as I had willingly given them my mobile number, but I honestly thought they'd just use it for arranging viewings.

We'd been house-hunting for ages and every time my text-beep went off, I thought it might be my girlfriend to say she'd found something suitable. That just doubled my disappointment when I discovered it was another poor match from the estate agent. It felt like being spammed on your phone.

In the end we found our house through another agent'.

According to...

Surinder Hundal – Nokia

'In Finland, mobile phone ownership is almost 100% and people do develop a sort of relationship with their mobile. I talk to teenage children in Finland and they say they feel naked without their phone; they would rather lose their set of house keys than their phone. They said when they leave the house the first thing they pick up is their phone, then their wallet or purse and keys'.

We also need to understand the 'physical limitations' of texting, if we are to get the most from it. There is finite size of text message we can realistically compose because of the small screen sizes and the need to scroll.

At it's best, a text message should be some kind of alert, like an invitation, an announcement or offer. Before you decide to send a business text, think about the benefits:

Texting is very personal – it's often used by people with close relationships

Texting is quick – great as a follow up to more formal communication

Texting is succinct – it gets simple messages across effectively

Texting is incisive – it cuts through the 'noise' of other communications

Here are some examples of good use of text in business situations.

To say 'well done' to a member of your team

To announce a result – 'we won the sales pitch'

To empathise with a colleague – 'sorry your day isn't working out!'

To impart information – 'yes, Friday at noon is fine by me!'

We don't recommend using text to say 'you're sacked!', although cases where this has occurred have made national headlines in the past.

According to...

Surinder Hundal – Nokia

'Because texting someone is more remote than a face-to-face meeting, managers may feel it's an easier way of delivering bad news – you don't have to look into the 'whites of their eyes', so you feel you can get away with delivering the bad news without having to think what the repercussions would be'.

So, balance the pros and cons if you're thinking of using text as a business tool. Without doubt it's set to become more and more popular, but heed the warnings above before you launch headlong into arranging all your meetings on it, or announcing 10% discount day to all your customers.

Finally we turn again to Surinder Hundal of Nokia.

The Expert Panel

Surinder Hundal
Nokia

'We are continually having conversations within Nokia about the social impact of what we do but sometimes you can't be sure what that'll be in advance. Take texting for example, when we developed that, we thought it wouldn't be used very much, but even if it was it would mainly be for business applications, like maybe checking people's availability if you were setting up a meeting – and now you get something like 8 billion text messages a month globally.

What's interesting is that quite a lot of the traffic is in messages that aren't substantive. It's almost like the equivalent of speech, people are conversing with each other through text and that is obviously a change in social behaviour.

Within Nokia we've found text really useful, particularly as an alert, so you might want to alert people to results being announced or signposting some news that might be appearing on email or the intranet, so it's really a broadcast method'.

Writing for the Internet

You might not have to write web copy but this topic will help develop your communication skills for two reasons.

Firstly, by understanding what is good and bad practice in web-writing, you will be better able to judge how much another organisation knows or cares about its internet presence. Apart from this, the disciplines of writing good web copy can teach us a lot about how to present other forms of written work to get the maximum attention and response from our audience.

Why the Internet is different

Our increasing usage of the Internet has led us to discover a number of key differences in the way it is consumed.

Paradoxically, it's slow! – reading speeds are significantly diminished from a computer screen, some say by up to 30%. A number of theories have been put forward why this is. Certainly it's partly down to the quality of the type, a good printer turning out high resolution hard copy will provide you with documents that are much easier to read, but web *design* has an influence too. Often there's a lot of distracting clutter on a web page that draws our eye away from the text and makes it difficult to concentrate.

And it gets slower. There are a couple of other simple but practical reasons for us slowing down; firstly, many sites are still too complex in their structure and may even use long passages of text which need to be scrolled through. Turning a page is much quicker.

Usage – think about what you use the Internet for. Is it for research, monitoring competitors, information, fun, leisure, online booking or banking, news and weather? The list goes on. In all these cases a degree of surfing will probably be necessary meaning we'll skip lightly from one page to another, from one site to the next, taking little time to stop and read anything in detail. That makes the demands on the writing style all the more significant, if we are to hold people at our site.

Mindset – there's a world of difference between setting some time aside to read a 100 page report that's landed on your desk, and the way that we hop in and out of cyberspace. How many times have you used the phrase, 'I'll just have a quick look on the Internet'. Now you can see the difference in how your concentration level will be for each task. Under those circumstances you have to be able to hit visitors to your own site hard and fast, give them what they want in the shortest time possible and allow them to move on.

Competitive time pressure – given the information overload that we are all subject to, we often have to resort to reading just a summary of everything we see. This has resulted in something of a 'sound bite' culture, but its increasing inevitability means that web pages need to keep pace. Because the Internet is so vast and there are many competing sites for every type of need, we no longer have to stick with something, to see if it delivers what we're looking for. If a page downloads too slowly, has poor navigation, looks untidy or fails within milliseconds to offer us the information we're looking for, then we're off searching elsewhere.

Learn how to overcome much of this with tight copy and you will have become an expert in succinct, informative, entertaining writing. The techniques are simple.

Upside down – we believe it's best to write web copy in an 'inverted pyramid style', with the most important information at the top and the detail further down. This is also true of newspaper stories and advertisements. The starting point is to get the essence of the story, or offer, or information across as quickly as possible, if you like it's a kind of headline. Based on this, people will make an instant decision whether to read on or go elsewhere, so it's important to get it right.

Scan-tastic! – there's lots of evidence to suggest people don't sit and read every word of web copy, but simply scan through it to get the essence of what is being said. You can make this much easier for them if you think about layout, and try to use as much white space as possible; it really does make for easier reading. If you're working alongside a good web designer, they will do this as a matter of course, blending your words in with their graphics and images.

Sum it up – bullet points are a great way of summarising what you're saying. You could start with a couple of opening paragraphs and then go on to summarise in bullet form the core of the story or the benefits of your offer. Needless to say the bullets should be pithy and to the point.

No ramblers here! – long sentences that seem to go nowhere are out. What you need are lots of short sentences that say what needs to be said. For some reason this style is much easier to read. The extra benefit is that people will remember more of what you've said.

When you've finished writing your web copy, is it all of these things?

Understandable – at a glance
Concise – half as many words as for any other medium
Simple – Plain English
Relevant – to what you'd promised

<u>Loaded with bullets</u>

Bullet point lists are commonplace, but often poorly constructed. Here are some hints on how to make your bullets better. Firstly, remember that the list should be centred around a single theme, so it might be a collection of reasons to support an argument, or it could be something as simple as a list of names or statements.

For design reasons your bullets should be roughly the same length. This also makes them easier to digest. It doesn't matter if you use upper or lower case, or end with a full stop or not, as long as you're consistent.

Bullet points should be used when you have a list of items all of which carry equal weight or importance.

If your text relies on a logical sequence, like instructions or directions, you should use a numbered list rather than bullet points indicating that the points need to be followed in order.

You can adopt or adapt many of these web-writing tips and use them across the spectrum of your written communication, you'll certainly find what you're producing is more concise. Check with a mentor or your peers to see if people like what and how you've written your copy, feedback is a great way of improving.

The Elevator Test for Chapter 6

- Email is now the most common form of written communication so treat it with respect and learn to use it well

- Make sure the email you send is RELEVANT to the audience, keep it short and to the point

- Don't get drawn into a war of words on email. If there's a conflict situation, sort it out face-to-face

- Of all new technologies, text messaging is the most personal and intimate

- Texting is good as an alert mechanism, but use it sparingly

- Writing for the Internet requires discipline and, at most, only half the words of other written communications

- Users only tend to scan web pages, so messages need to be punchy and design is best kept simple

CHAPTER 7

New technologies – new rules, old adages

Writing a chapter on technology is a sure fire way of making a book look dated within a matter of months, or is that minutes? The tools we use change with such frightening frequency, it is likely you'll be using a new device or channel before this ink has dried.

As far back as the nineties, in the highly competitive market of portable stereo, Sony had reduced the product life cycle to 12 weeks. If you had just bought the latest version of a digital Walkman (even the word seems dated now), at your high street store in Europe, it was already obsolete in Japan and had been replaced with an updated model, rich with new features.

The world has changed even more dramatically since, both in terms of the hardware we use and the communication channels that are now open. Smart phones and tablets take us one step further away from needing an office, and it is only the face-to-face connectedness, the social side of work, which binds it together. The filing cabinets full of text, drawings, quotations, financial records, images and even video have been shrunk into a mobile device which we can use virtually anywhere. Even the connectivity issues of a few years ago, seem to be fading, and we must surely soon have a 'wireless world' where we can roam free and be 'always on'.

Before we sort through the communication issues this raises for us as individuals, let's take a brief look at some of the big changes of the last ten years.

Blogging

We need to go back one step further in the evolution of the internet to get a perspective on how blogging (short for web logging), came into being and achieved such popularity. In the early years of the internet, only those with the unique skill of being able to write html code (the instructions that operate 'behind' what we see), could develop websites. When more user friendly software was developed, allowing intuitive cut and paste, drag and drop or click and build solutions, suddenly having a personal web site was no longer a novelty. The difficulty which arose next was how to drive traffic to your site, and keep it 'sticky'. This meant getting users to hang around a while or return on a regular basis. Frequent updates of content were clearly necessary, and blogging allowed us to accomplish this. It also gave individuals a voice, one which they could 'broadcast' to as wide an audience as was interested.

Although many bloggers use the tool as a way of cataloguing their day-to-day experiences, with no other purpose than to entertain, there are others who take a journalistic approach, reporting, or passing comment upon more serious events in the current affairs arena. To their audience, they are often seen as a refreshing counterpoint to more established journalism, they are regarded as opinion-formers.

Anyone with their own site can start a blog, but it helps if you have an opinion worth listening to, and the time on your hands to sustain the output.

Social media

Currently Facebook is in vogue, a year or two ago it was Myspace and Bebo, but nothing stays still for very long on the internet. Whatever the most popular site is, they are all underpinned by the core principle of linking up like-minded people, to chat, share, form groups and state opinions.

The 'nay-sayers of social media' will point to examples of users with hundreds of yet-unmet friends. These are individuals who have stumbled across each other, through chains of friends of a friend, of a friend etc., or those who completely independently, have expressed common interest over an issue or event and added each other to their database. 'Friends' has simply become an over-arching term for this kind of relationship, they're not the people who would drag you out of a burning building, but still there is a connection. The fact you have never met is an irrelevance.

Social media is powered by acquaintance.

Microblogging

The nature of the evolution of the technologies we have just dis-cussed, means we are faced with coming to terms with a form of communication so dynamic, it changes all the while. For that reason, we have reserved a separate section for the analysis of microblogging, or to give it a more familiar title, Twitter.

Of course it is not true that Twitter is the only microblogging site, but it has achieved the same status in its own sphere as Google has in the search engine world. Twitter began life as an attempt to link small groups of like-minded individuals together, with snappy messages and updates. Although con-strained by it's 140 character limit, this has been more than compensated for by Twitter's unique and powerful appeal, which is that it operates in real time.

Implications

The nuts and bolts (or chips and circuits), of these new tech-nologies are the driving force behind being able to communicate more often, to different audiences in real time, but what are the wider implications, in social and business terms, how does the nature of our communication alter?

Speed is increasing, the truth might suffer

The escalating demand for 24 hour news and information sets a template which organisations and even individuals feel the need to follow. We may be drawn into giving quick answers because that is what others demand, but if we haven't had time to check the facts or analyse the data, our first reaction may turn out to be flawed.

According to…

Chris Lewis – Chris Lewis PR

'When it comes to reporting stories, it's always been the case that speed has been inverse to truth, so the faster a story operates, the less truth one can associate with it. If you're prepared to wait for ten years the truth will eventually emerge. If you want to wait for five years then the forensic scientists could tell you. In a couple of years the authors can tell you, in a matter of weeks the journalists will tell you, in days the blogs will tell you and in minutes the twitterers will tell you. So at each stage there is a widespread assumption that the validity of news stories remains unchanged, but it is changed dramatically by the speed at which they flow'.

We're all interconnected

One-to-one communication is still desperately important in business, but one-to-many can be just as significant. New technologies have given us the ability to swiftly build a web of interconnected contacts, who we might seek to influence. In the same way by accepting *incoming* requests, we place our-selves into others' networks, often without thinking through the implications.

This opens up a myriad of exciting new possibilities, like the phenomenon of 'crowdsourcing', where the skills and abilities of a disparate audience are tapped into to solve a problem. The masses can be galvanised in pursuit of other aims too, like changing everything from the nature of the pop charts to the entire political system of whole countries. Canny marketers have witnessed this power too, attempting to launch viral campaigns for their products, where the word is spread (like a virus), from one online user to another, importantly at zero cost.

All businesses need to wake up to the fact that their customers are more in control than ever.

According to...

Kevin Roberts – Saatchi and Saatchi

'Most companies are in the middle of a revolution, even when they don't know it, because power has switched, irrespective of what business you are in from brands, from retail, into the hands of consumers and most companies haven't got a clue what's going on. So revolution is in the air, because consumers are revolting'.

Networks have increased in size

Our opinion is important. In many ways this has always been the case. It is our completely unique set of attributes which make us appealing to an employer. Opinions formed over a number of years and drawing on a host of diverse experiences are part of what makes us different. However, now we can make those views accessible to a much wider audience. Starting with a small local network, we can begin to influence and provoke the thoughts of a select, hand-picked group, then, if those opinions get noticed, we can begin to influence others further afield. Some of the best respected news bloggers have built their own audience of thousands, who follow their every word.

To be a successful communicator, we need to understand the power of these tools and treat them seriously and responsibly. One of the criticisms levelled at many young revellers today is that they happily post opinions, and even ill judged photographs of themselves online, believing only the few, within their circle of friends (real or virtual), will be interested. Some evidence has already emerged of companies searching online for the names of job applicants to get an insight into their lives. Some view this as unethical, but if we post online without considering security, we have voluntarily put ourselves in the public domain.

You have to wade through the rubbish

We are all suffering from 'information overload'. The sheer volume of data being forced upon us has been likened to 'drinking from a fire hose', a great analogy which expresses the difficulty we all face. If this is bad now, it is set to get worse as the growth of usage of these tools ramps up inexorably. Already analysts have begun to look at the nature of content, with some concluding that as much as 80% can be classified as 'conversation' or 'pointless babble', perhaps the age old 80:20 rule is going to apply here as elsewhere. Of course there is nothing wrong with either category in its place, after all we are forever hearing 'it's good to talk', but it does make the job of filtering what we listen to harder than ever.

There is no arbiter of truth, or sometimes decency

If we think our opinion is important then we equally need to accept that others are entitled to theirs too. Social networks, which put the power of communication in our hands, do exactly the same for all the other players, even those who we violently disagree with, For this reason, we need to accept that not everything we read will be to our taste, some of it may be wholly inaccurate, or even malicious.

As consumers of this kind of messaging, this inevitably leads us to a point where we need to filter what is 'out there', but entitles our potential audience to do the same.

There are no longer a few 'controlling' players

So called 'mass media' was once in control of what we saw or heard. In the right hands, this has been a good thing, with issues of taste, decency, honesty and integrity being at the heart of many news organisations. That said, in more controlling regimes, this power has sometimes been exploited for political, corrupt or propaganda purposes.

What has changed is that now any of us can become a 'mass media' outlet, as long as we are able to garner enough followers. Large audiences are naturally drawn to celebrities, but aside from this modern fascination with the lives of the famous, there are countless examples of lone, unknown individuals attracting a large and faithful following, simply because their opinions resonate with a wide public.

It would be easy under circumstances of such massive change to be frightened for the future, but perhaps we should console ourselves with the words of a communicator at the cutting edge of advertising.

According to...

Kevin Roberts – Saatchi and Saatchi

'Here's what I think, "plus ça change, plus ça meme chose. The more things change the more they stay the same" and I think that's a big headline because what's changed is technology. What hasn't changed is humanity'.

What does the future hold?

If we were able to predict with any certainty what the next stage of development of interconnected social media is, we could retire to that Caribbean island right now! Opinion is divided, with some saying the fad will pass and others proclaiming we are simply on a low rung of a ladder which will see our world as one joined up entity, giving us all the opportunity to express our opinion or vote upon every issue.

Whichever side is right, there are still some unshakeable foundations of communication which look unlikely to be moved. The first is that old cliché which says 'content is king'. More and more it matters both 'what' you say and 'how' you say it. Choosing which channel to 'broadcast' on is significant, but if the message is all wrong, you can pump it out to the world again and again, without it ever making an impact.

How to use social media

As with all other forms of communication there is a set of 'best practice' associated with the newest of channels. Getting the best out of the technology can help you and your organisation gain and sustain competitive advantage.

According to…

Chris Lewis – Chris Lewis PR

'Of course there are lots of organisations that don't even know of the existence of microblogging. They think Twitter is really there for teenagers to say which coffee shop they're in. You get forward thinking organisations, who don't accept the world is standing still, they see its progress very rapidly from the bottom up and the "digital natives" that are coming into their stores. Aged 15 or 16, they've never known anything else. Sadly, most Boards are constituted of people who are "digital immigrants" and they're trying to work out what the "digital natives" are doing. For modern corporations social media can be used as a sword as well as a shield. It can be used as sword in terms of customer service and being able to enhance the way customers interact but it can also be used as a shield to quickly counter a complaint.'

Multiple identities

There are many facets to our character, and we show different faces to the world according to our circumstances. At a job interview, we may not decide to talk up our addiction to extreme sports or model railway collecting, it's about appropriateness. In the same way, it is better to avoid putting all your communication eggs in one basket. Choose different tools for each aspect of your life you want to talk about. Twitter is a good general vehicle for more personal posts, but you might think about having a separate business presence on a site like LinkedIn.

Think content

If you have nothing intelligent or interesting to say, say nothing. This rule puts an onus on us to come up with content which is worth reading. Think back to the 'fire hose' analogy and it gives you the impetus to construct messages which will really stand out from the crowd. It is hard to be consistent with this, but if our standards slip, it won't be long before our audience will begin to tune out and find something which is more to their taste.

Little and often

The busy lives we lead necessitate taking on board lots of different information and influences as quickly as we can, and this in turn requires us, when in the role of the sender, to master the art of 'short messaging', it really is a case where less is more. Pithy, informative updates, regularly despatched are much more likely to grab attention. Think of a blog as an online diary, something which requires frequent updates.

As in many spheres of modern life, we can be forgotten all too soon if we don't remind people we are still around. A blog which you update once a month is unlikely to sustain much of an audience.

Tease

Conventional broadcast media, like radio and television are constantly reminding us of what is 'coming up next' in order to whet our appetites. The best websites do the same thing, encouraging us with an engaging headline, to click through for 'the good stuff'. Apply this technique to your outgoing messages; give people something to 'look forward to', and you will achieve the same aim. 'Stickiness', or getting people to stay with you, rather than search elsewhere, is one of the key aims of all good broadcasters, whatever delivery medium they are using.

Think twice

Before you press 'send' take a moment to read what you have written and consider it from the perspective of the intended audience. There are two parties to any communication, the sender and the receiver, so just because you have something to express, there is no guarantee it will engage the other party. The same rules apply here as with any outgoing message, is it well constructed, does it say what you want it to and have you phrased it in a way which will appeal to the receiver?

Although the above protocols are widely recognised as being a common sense approach to using social media, the phenomenon is evolving all the time and for each of us, a degree of trial and error will be necessary to get the best out of it. In the early days, keep track of what works for you and try to analyse the reasons behind your successes, then simply follow that line.

We have recognised that the future is difficult to predict in this area, but what does seem to be emerging is the need for 'smart filtering'. Just as our digital television recorder can begin to recognise patterns and suggest content and our music download sites predict what we will like according to the patterns of other users who have similar profiles to us, social media looks set to go this way.

None of us can possibly monitor everything which is being posted and in order to access the topics we are interested in, we are going to need some digital help. All of this brings us neatly back to the importance of content, only by producing our own rich, interesting, engaging messages, will we stand a chance of getting through the filters of our target audience.

The Elevator Test for Chapter 7

- Technology is ever-changing, it's pace is ever-increasing

- Your opinion is important, think carefully about how you express it

- Social media moves us on from one-to-one. Now we can communicate one-to-many

- Respect these new channels; think twice before pressing 'send'

- Content has, is, and will always be the most important part of *any* communication

CHAPTER 8

Listening

Now we've examined the elements of the written word, it's time to move on and look at something we do instinctively and naturally, every day of our lives, 'listening' and 'talking'. As with other aspects of communication we've discussed, we aim to take this subject and move it into a more conscious state, so you can analyse and improve on the way you do it now.

We'll then look at how to apply what we have learned to increase the effectiveness of what we say, and the usefulness of what we hear. Included in this will be sections on how to conduct phone conversations, what to look out for in meetings and ways of presenting to small or large audiences that will get your message across in a more persuasive way.

How to listen

> *'If you listen to everything that you hear, not just the words, but what's going on around them you get a much richer picture'.*
>
> Simon Armson – The Samaritans

Why don't we listen more?

According to...

John Akers – Relationship Counsellor

'Most of us are not brought up to be very good listeners.

In your childhood you often come away with a sense of criticism, you come through school there's lots of criticism, in your job there's lots of criticism and I think a lot of people become very defensive unless they're very sure of themselves.

You have to find a way of allowing people to be vulnerable without it being fatal, so that people have the opportunity to grow up and change'.

General rules of listening

We deal with listening before talking for a very good reason and that's because the former informs the latter, in other words, what we say is usually governed by what has gone before. Understanding the other party's point of view helps us respond appropriately.

In addition, appearing to listen properly has the dual benefit of making the other person feel valued, while giving you enough time to formulate a suitable response. Just think how useful this technique will be in a formal interview situation. Sometimes, we feign interest, believing it is the polite thing to do. However, it would be stupid to suggest that other people aren't able to pick up on this as the following anecdote shows.

A Good Story

The monthly management meeting always dragged on longer than it should, and the low spot was a presentation of the sales figures by Roger the Head of Finance.

The rest of the attendees tried their very hardest to look interested, but with his dull monotone, meticulous detail and lack of humour it was a trial.

After one such meeting the Head of Operations approached the Marketing Director and said, 'I saw you this afternoon during Roger's presentation; you were operating on vital organs only'.

Maybe you can relate to that feeling?

If you are faced with a similar scenario, in a regularly scheduled meeting, try to manage the situation rather than waste the time. If you have sufficient influence (i.e. if you are the line manager of the culprit), then think about some suitable coaching, either from yourself or a third party.

If your influence is more limited then look at ways of changing behaviours. You could lead by example, producing a sparkling and interesting report when it's your turn, or ask interesting questions to the other party to break the monotony.

Phrasing can be important here too; don't belittle their area of responsibility, but find an appropriate way of eliciting the information you need. Here's an example.

'Roger, could you just give us the overall group figures and the reasons why they appear to be down – you can email the individual area numbers to us later, to digest in our own time'.

With a little forethought, we can come up with a form of words which will influence, but not offend the other party.

Natural interest

When we truly are interested in what someone has to say we send out lots of non-verbal signals in an unconscious way. It follows therefore, that if you consciously mimic those actions when someone is talking, they will naturally think that you are enchanted with what they are saying. Journalists, salesmen and suitors are all great at adopting this high attention behaviour. This is a good short term technique, but because it requires a lot of concentration, it's difficult to keep it up for long periods.

The natural behaviours of attentiveness look like the following:

Make eye contact
Lean forward
Mirror the speaker's actions and mannerisms
Keep your pose open
Signal frequent agreement (by nodding and smiling)

Eye contact is vitally important in making the other party aware of how interested you are; it is important in social situations and just as significant in business. We tend to judge people who won't meet our gaze as shifty and untrustworthy, but also be aware that using too much eye contact can be threatening in some situations, so try to be sensitive to the response you are getting.

Another important element of body language involves leaning in towards the speaker, as if attempting to ensure you don't miss a single syllable of what they are saying. Be careful to make sure that all the signals are matching up, for maximum impact.

Mirroring is the curious ritual we engage in which involves copying the other party in everything they do, we often do it without knowing. It shows empathy in an unconscious way and signals our approval of them as an individual and of their actions. Once again, with concentration we can do this consciously but don't make it too obvious or the other person will begin to wonder what you are doing.

Crossed legs or arms or a 'bunched' pose, shows you are on the defensive, maybe even intimidated or afraid. Learn to relax and keep your arms and legs loose, rather than wound around each other.

If you ever watch a radio or television interview being conducted, you will see the journalist frantically and frequently nodding their agreement to keep their guest talking. They may even occasionally verbalise this with a grunt of assent, an 'I see' or a 'how interesting' type of phrase.

In many situations we feel duty bound to fill any silence which falls, but don't be too hasty. Silence can be a very powerful tool in getting another person to open up. Rather than always jumping in with an opinion of our own, we can often elicit much more detail from people if we are prepared to leave a gap.

When we're genuinely animated about what someone else is saying, we show our approval by smiling. Coupled with the nodding technique above, this is an irresistible signal to most speakers to keep them feeling that they are delivering awe-inspiring thoughts.

There are lots of situations where using this behaviour is helpful, including job interviews, sales pitches and meetings. It is also a recognised part of the process of coaching. There's nothing fake or phoney either, it's simply about understanding how to get the other party to open up.

In some extreme situations, the ability to listen can even be a matter of life and death. That's the case for the charity The Samaritans

The Expert Panel

Simon Armson
The Samaritans

'Any communication is a three-part process, there's a transmission, then there's the medium through which the message is transmitted and finally, there's the reception.

As far as the Samaritans communication is concerned what is absolutely paramount is the ability to listen and to hear, and to be able to hear not only what's said on the lines, as it were, but also what's said *between* the lines.

A lot of work is done on the telephone and it surprises many people the amount of non-verbal communication that takes place on the telephone. One has to be very attuned to that, so one's hearing and listening skills have to be very carefully honed.

I think listening and hearing are two different things. You can listen by actually hearing, I don't mean just reacting to the sound waves that enter your ear, but actually hearing what's meant, what's expressed, what's not said, what the emotions are, what the feelings are that are contained within the words which you are actually listening to.

When you're on the telephone it's not just the sounds that you hear, it's the silences too, it's the noises that you hear, that aren't words, but are maybe to do with breathing, maybe to do with crying, it maybe to do with sighing, it maybe to do with the external environment, so you can detect where someone is. Are they on the street, are they in a call box are they in their home? Have they got the radio and television on? Is there a pet in the vicinity? Those sort of things help you build a picture.

So I think there's an important distinction between the act of listening which is a sort of passive act, it happens because you've got ears that work, whereas hearing is something which I believe you have to work at'.

When to listen

'Shut up! – for every minute that you talk, spend two listening'
                                        Professor David Clutterbuck

It wouldn't be natural if we tried to listen with this high degree of attentiveness all the time, nor would it be appropriate in all circumstances. The amount of concentration we devote to our listening is often tuned to the importance of the circumstance. We listen attentively to instructions or important news, much more passively to the radio or general conversation.

Most business situations fluctuate between these two extremes; the trick is to decide where each individual conversation lies. Clearly the amount of attention you should give to any situation should be directly related to its potential significance. You can make your own list of criteria based on your job description and department, then add that to the four situations below.

First meeting
Negotiation

Announcements
Hierarchical

A first meeting, with a new client or supplier, or even with other departments in your own organisation is critical in establishing the balance of power and the foundations of a relationship, so you must pay a lot of attention. Beyond that, any circumstance when negotiation is going to take place is an important one from a listening point of view.

Announcements need to be heeded and digested carefully, as you may be part of the cascade process and need to interpret what is being said so you can outline the implications to peers or your own team. 'Hierarchical listening' is as simple as making sure you pay attention when the boss is speaking!

Of course, you shouldn't devote your attention solely to these situations, this is not permission to switch off when anybody else is talking. What we are saying is that there are some situations that demand your special attention. Anticipating what they are in advance means you are more likely to tune in properly when they take place.

Certainly the mark of successful communicators is their ability to take a step back from a situation and listen to what's being said.

According to…

Simon Terrington – Human Capital

'How much you listen and how you listen, then how much you talk and how you talk are just a fascinating balance. Confident and successful people tend to listen.

I'll give you an example, a kid is struggling at school and the kid will say "Dad I hate school" and the dad will straightaway go into autobiography "When I was a lad, I worked hard, I was top of my class at maths, went on to get top grades in my exams…" and the kid just looks on in desperation.

And what the Dad needs to say is "You're having a bad time at school?" and the kid can say "Yeah, I just don't know what

I'm doing in science" or "I can't understand the teacher", and if you have a chat about it and find out what's going on. Then you can actually diagnose the problem and start prescribing a solution. But the idea that you'd walk into the Doctors and he'd say "Here you go, these drugs will get you better, good-bye!" before you've even said what's wrong is ludicrous'.

The Elevator Test for Chapter 8

- Listening is nearly always more important than speaking

- Hear what others have to say first, it'll help you formulate a better response

- Learn the techniques of being attentive, apply them in appropriate circumstances

- Shut up and listen! – for every minute that you talk, spend two listening

- Avoid the temptation to jump in with solutions, when you haven't fully explored the problem

CHAPTER 9

Talking

'The ability to talk rather than write is very important, because you can communicate a message far more power- fully using voice rather than text. You get away with a lot more by speaking, just the inflection in your voice can reveal how you're feeling'.

Russell Grossman – BBC

Spoken word can be the most powerful way of communicating, so in this chapter we're going to examine both the message and the delivery method. We'll start with what you say, then con- sider the best way of putting it across. Because talking is such a frequently used communication tool, perhaps our principal method of making our feelings known, it is often overlooked as we take it for granted.

However, there are very few people who have the natural ability to cut all the waffle from their speech and 'package' what they say into persuasive, coherent, compelling phrases. Perhaps the exception to this is the politician, many of whom have trained themselves to speak in this way, knowing that in this media age, delivering a sound bite in front of the cameras will increase the likelihood of it being 'aired'.

For the rest of us, the natural 'uums', 'errms', false starts and changes of direction mid sentence are part of how we speak. Eradicate some of this and you will sound much more com- pelling, but it takes work, a raising of consciousness and maybe most difficult of all, a good deal of thought before we open our mouths!

Spoken content

Whatever your message is, try to get into the habit of chunking it into a maximum of three components.

The theory of 'lists of 3' has been examined many times. Politicians and orators use it over and over again when speaking, keeping their message within the confines of a three point plan. There are two ways of looking at this (though it would fit better if there were three!). We all know that attention spans are limited and it seems that the more information overload we face the worse it gets. Even hard news programmes are forced into cutting items down to bite-sized pieces for us to consume.

The second issue is this. In the mind of the listener, the illusion of brevity makes us pay greater attention. If we have been told at the beginning there are only three main points to follow, most of us can cope with keeping our attention high. Contrast this with a speaker who says they're about to outline their 12 point plan, we know we are not going to be able to retain it all, so tend to tune out right away.

'Three' is about the most we want to have to cope with.

If this seems inconvenient because you have just finished drawing up your intricate plan for success, then you should think about how you could present it as being a three stage plan, each of which has a number of sub-sections.

When you sit down to formulate your message, you need to put yourself in the position of the listener; how will your communication be decoded and consumed? What you say will be governed by many factors, some of which are listed below. You will be able to add your own according to the type of organisation you work for.

How much do you know?
Who else needs to know?
How much do you need to tell them?
Is there sensitive or confidential material?
What will be the impact (on morale? on the way we operate?)

Is there any commercial sensitivity?

How important is timing?

What is the balance of risk? (saying nothing can sometimes be dangerous)

Learn from the people around you including your boss, your peers, your staff. Only you can decide where to draw the lines, but think about where honesty fits in? At what point does genuine concern for others, lapse into a desire to gossip about their private life? What impact does an unhealthy secrecy have on other people?

How you say it

> *'I think it's a good idea to come up with a single sentence on any project you're involved with. It's a great way of making sure you're able to deliver the message very quickly and it has the added benefit that it focuses your own mind'.*
>
> Professor Cary Cooper

Once you have decided on what the message is, how do you put it across? You need to consider both the form of words you choose, and the physical elements of delivery. The starting point is to distil the message down to its bare essentials, in much the same way as we've done in the 'elevator test' summaries at the end of each chapter.

This tends to focus your attention on what is really important; it's a great way of honing your messages into their core elements.

Some of the most effective communicators decide on their message in advance of any communication and then deliver it relentlessly. Senior managers in many organisations undergo media training, to help them cope in such situations. Irrespective of the issue that's being discussed, they will tell you how that relates to the way things are done in their company.

Listen carefully to politicians being interviewed and it's rare for them to answer the question with anything other than the message they want to get across. This is how it's done.

According to…

> Derek Hatton – Broadcaster and former Politician
>
> 'If you're being interviewed for tonight's news and you know that there's one single point you want to make you have to focus on that. Let's say the point you want to put across is, "the shirt I am going to wear is black", then it goes like this…
>
> "But Mr. Hatton, why was it that when you did that, there was an immediate drop in the share price?"
>
> "The shirt that I'm going to wear is black"
>
> "But Mr. Hatton why is it that Everton didn't get into Europe?"
>
> "The shirt that I'm going to wear is black"
>
> When that reporter gets back to the studio and his editor says "what have you got?" he'll say "I've got, the shirt he wants to wear is black".
>
> "What?!" says the editor, "Well if that's all you've got, then I'll have to use it"'.

It may be that under many mundane circumstances you just need to get on with delivering what you have to say in the most succinct and matter of fact way, there may be little room for window-dressing. However, some types of message may need extra impact and then it's worth considering a more 'theatrical' approach. Sometimes this is also dependent on the surroundings and nature of the presentation.

In a one-to-one or small meeting, the measured, succinct delivery of the politician would be appropriate, but if your task is to galvanise, motivate or inspire a larger group of people, say at a conference, a touch of additional dramatic input may be required. You might think about using some of the following techniques:

Comedy
Drama
Suspense
Mystery
Action
Thrills

If you want to study these aspects of 'engagement' in greater detail, then think about them when you next watch a movie or a live theatre show, and ask yourself, what it is about the performance which inspires particular feelings within you. Why do you feel scared, tense, happy, moved? What is happening within the piece to spark these emotions? A greater awareness and understanding will help you emulate these techniques in your own 'performance'.

As with all forms of communication, we need to take heed of the type of audience we are addressing and consider their level of familiarity with the topic, the mix of gender, their average age and the level they've reached within the organisation. Try hard to imagine what it's like for them receiving the message, and you'll get a much better feel for if you've pitched it right.

Rehearsed and unrehearsed speech

Of course, in real life not everything is so well considered. Don't get too concerned with thinking you can never again open your mouth to speak without first having run the up and coming sentence through a rigorous vetting process. We indulge in 'unrehearsed speech' all the time, it's part of our daily lives, an instinctive reaction to what is going on around us. We use it for much of our day-to-day business dealings too. We give our opinions, pass on knowledge and respond to the ever-changing situations we encounter. The only thing we would urge when it comes to this type of communication is that once in a while you stop and think about how you sound.

Are you satisfied that you always come across in the way you intended, or do you sometimes feel your words or meaning are misconstrued? Being aware of how you sound, and sensitive to how your audience may interpret your messages, will go a long way towards making you a great communicator.

At the other extreme, there is the meticulously planned and well-rehearsed presentation. You may have repeated this to yourself many times, even in front a trusted colleague and will have had an opportunity to apply a more rigorous and objective set of criteria to what you're saying and the way you're saying it. But in between there are many more occasions when you can think carefully about your message and rehearse what you are going to say in your head.

A quiet five minutes before the start of a meeting to review your notes, and visualise how you will deliver them, will go a long way to making you more articulate and sure of your ground.

The Elevator Test for Chapter 9

- Because the voice can convey so much, it's easier to persuade through talking than writing

- Sticking to lists of 'three' helps audiences grasp your message more easily and makes content easier to remember

- Think hard about your target audience, what they'll need or want to know, how they'll respond to what you say

- Distil your core message down to its shortest form. Think about what it is you're *really* saying

- Theatrical techniques can bring your speech to life. Make sure the context is appropriate

- Occasionally try to hear yourself as other people hear you and analyse how you sound

CHAPTER 10

Listening and talking – the rules of the tools

When talking and listening come together.

Sometimes we listen, sometimes we talk, mostly we do both.

Now we're going to examine the difference between face-to-face communication, and occasions when you can't see the other party, like during a telephone conversation.

What's the difference?

Communication is a two way process, and in order to be more effective at sending 'messages' to the other party, we need to be sensitive to how they are receiving them. What people say out loud does not always tie up with how they feel inside.

Relate

The marriage guidance service has a mass of experience of people failing in their communication. You ask your partner, 'how are you?' and get the answer, 'fine!' but is it borne out in their body language? The chances are you know right away if things aren't okay. The mismatch between verbal and non-verbal messages stands out a mile.

Tone of voice, posture, facial expression and lack of eye contact can all be signs that things are far from 'fine'. Under these circumstances you have to deal with the entirety of the communication and not just what is being verbalised. Failing to do so can soon lead to bigger problems if the issue is not addressed early. Failing to tackle the issues can lead to a spiral of non-communication to the point where two people involved can no longer relate to each other at all.

The specialist help of marriage guidance is often called upon just to get the parties talking again, to teach them how to communicate. This is the starting point to re-building what has gone wrong.

According to…

> John Akers – Relationship Counsellor
>
> 'Listening and talking are very important because I would say that largely speaking, poor communication is one of the main reasons why relationships breakdown'.

When we can see people reacting to what we are saying we have more clues to how they are actually feeling and can adapt as we go, in order to get the outcome we want. The telephone doesn't allow us to do that, but in certain circumstances people can become attuned to the mood of the other party, simply by experience of listening and talking to many people on the phone.

Think about what Simon Armson of The Samaritans, said, 'it's not just what is on the lines, but between the lines' which is important. We need to hone our listening skills to pick up these signals.

Of course The Samaritans are dealing with very serious issues, but the techniques they talk about can be applied in business to great effect. What you need are skilled operators who are sensitive to the mood and personality of their customers.

With this in mind, many call centres have developed a mantra which says recruit for attitude and train for skill. This means they get the right kind of people in the first place, and then equip them with the tools and training to do the job.

When service based companies get it right, this kind of real life scenario is the result.

A Good Story

A caller had conducted a number of routine banking transactions like paying bills and checking balances, and was pleased to hear that a particular large cheque had cleared leaving him with some financial security. He thought the call was over, when this happened.

OPERATOR: Just before you go Mr. May can I ask you a question?

CALLER: (expecting it to be some advice about how to invest the money) Yes, of course.

OPERATOR: I see from your account that a large sum has just been paid in and I was wondering...

CALLER: Yes?

OPERATOR: Will you marry me?!

The point of the story is that having the confidence to joke around with customers is borne out of the experience of being able to read them, in a particular situation. In this case, it was a mixture of evidence provided by the technology of the large balance, added to an assessment of the type of person the caller was (picked up during the early routine transactions), that made the operator take the risk of the joke. You can't train people for this kind of interaction, you have instead to select the right personalities and give them the freedom to use their discretion. The operator later confessed to the caller that she was happily married with five children!

For most of us, we take the telephone for granted, but we may not yet have the highly developed skill to use it with the effectiveness of a good call centre operator. How do we use the phone better and communicate more effectively with it?

The evolution of the culture surrounding telephone usage is a fascinating study of human behaviour. Prior to the growth of mobiles, the fixed line in many homes was connected to a telephone in the hall, often on a special telephone table. A call, outbound or inbound was an event!

Now, as part of the busy lives we lead, we take calls anywhere and everywhere. Phone 'etiquette' differs by nation and generation. Some top London restaurants take mobiles off people on the way in. By contrast, in Beijing it is not uncommon for people to not only take, but also instigate calls while eating with friends. Because of the every-dayness of this, we have become complacent over the power of the telephone.

There is also now an expectation that we are always available, we can no longer classify any telephone conversation as an event, it's just part of our daily lives.

To make the most of our telephone time, it is worth remembering the significant differences between inbound and outbound calls. What happens first of all when your phone rings?

You have little or no control over inbound calls – they can come at any time

You have no idea what to expect when you pick up the phone

With inbound calls the other party has set the agenda for discussion

Inbound calls are often disruptive to good time management

Because of these differences, you need to make provision in your working day to handle the situation. Again, technology looked like it had provided a solution, at least for a while. Now, however, we regard voicemail and voice activated menus as the scourge of our age, most of us just want to talk to a real person again! (There's advice on how to get the best from voicemail in the next chapter).

Some managers are in their office the whole day and rather than answer the phone and be interrupted, they leave voicemail on the whole time, vetting incoming calls or checking back now and again to see if anyone interesting enough to warrant a call back has phoned.

It is much better to learn how to 'handle' human beings who call, than to ignore them, and because you can never be sure what to expect when you pick up a ringing phone, you have to be prepared to cope with uncertainty.

Inbound calls

Here are some techniques for managing incoming calls as a necessary (in fact vital), part of your working day.

Don't let the incoming call control you, take the initiative and handle it with the right blend of efficiency and friendliness. The first thing you will establish is who the call is from. This gives you a chance to make a quick assessment of how to handle the conversation. How important is this person, are they usually quick and efficient or do they waffle on for hours? Is it likely they have a specific objective in mind, or do they sometimes call because they are trying to fill their day (most people have come across this type now and again).

Balance your assessment of the other party with a consideration of how much time you have? Sometimes it's good to take time to chat on the phone, you can find out a lot of important information this way and it helps to bind those important relationships together. If on the other hand, you've got a busy day you need to have your own techniques for cutting the conversation short.

Once you've established who is calling and how much time you have on your hands, get as quickly as possible to the point of the call. Now you're far more likely to be in control, by offering some options on how the enquiry can best be resolved.

With regular callers who have routine enquires that are important (without being urgent), you can ask that they always call you at a particular time ('You'll find it's easier to get me after about 4 p.m. My meetings have usually finished by then'), or even ask them to email you as you can then fit their enquiry into a time-managed email block.

Another strategy is to arrange call sharing with a close colleague and agree to answer the phones on an hour-by-hour basis. In this way, you can do some 'call filtering' e.g. 'if the boss rings then put them through, if it's Lynda in accounts, say I'll call her back'. There are two extra benefits to this; firstly your callers get a human being to speak to and, secondly, you can do some quick prioritisation before starting your call back session. It may be in some instances your colleague can answer the query on your behalf.

When you are pushed for time, you can cut them short politely.

You are probably already better at techniques for getting rid of people than you think. We all build up a stock of phrases and probably use them unwittingly when we are busy and need to get on.

'I'm sorry to interrupt you, but I'm really pressed for time at the moment...'

'To be honest it may be better if we saved this discussion until later, so that I've had a chance to think a bit more carefully about the issues...'

If you really want to stop someone mid flow, say their name, 'John, that's really interesting but...' and if you get desperate, the universal way to signal you've had enough is to say the word 'anyway'. It'll stop even the most talkative person in their tracks.

How to use voicemail

You'll have seen the merits of other technological advances discussed elsewhere in this book, but one tool seems to be disliked more than any other and that's voicemail. This is a little unfair, as it has many merits. Like lots of things, it is all about using it in the right way.

This section is about doing just that with as little pain, inconvenience and hassle as possible. Although it doesn't provide an instantaneous response to callers, voicemail can be a two-way exchange (on those days when you keep missing each other), so remember to look at it in terms of inbound and outbound communication.

It's important too to note that if you get it wrong at your end, you may be missing vital incoming messages. You will never know how many people hung up, just because you recorded a dull outgoing message!

Some of the merits of voicemail

It means we can 'answer' the phone when we're not around.

Callers get to hear a personal message from us

We can manage our time better

We can pick up messages remotely, so we don't need to return to the office

Callers save time and frustration by not having to call back

Callers can be sure that we'll actually get their message

Messages can be left out of normal office hours for action the following day

All of this sounds fine, and if voicemail wasn't so badly abused by so many users, then it would probably be judged as a good thing to have, a useful addition to the 'communications toolbox'.

As in so much communication, we can begin to improve only when we see the world from the perspective of the person we seek to communicate with. When these people ring, the thing they really want to do is to talk to you in person, it's you who can solve their problem, offer advice or help out. If you're not around then they would probably rather talk to someone who works with you, maybe a colleague who performs the same role. That would probably mean that they'd get some kind of an answer to their query. You might need to follow up at a later time to finalise details.

Next in the order of merit is the 'human message taker'. That is someone who is able to say that you are not at your workplace but who will pledge to make sure that the message is delivered.

At the bottom of the list comes voicemail. It seems there are still many people who dislike voicemail so much they refuse to leave a message, this is self-defeating as their frustration must surely be compounded when they have to call back a second time, only to be faced with the same voicemail message.

What we do need to recognise is that voicemail isn't top of everyone's list as a favourite communication tool, for many it is the last resort, when other attempts to get in touch have failed, for this reason, we need to make sure we use it as efficiently as we can.

Voicemail technique

The Do's

When you listen to some people's outgoing message you come away not knowing if or when they will ever return your call! Here's some advice on how to handle your outgoing message and what to include:

<u>Your name</u> – if they've not spoken to you before, how can they be sure they're through to the right person

<u>Your company</u> – especially if you have a phone system that allows outside callers to dial your phone direct. If they've dialled incorrectly at least they'll know they're through to the wrong organisation!

<u>The date</u> – you should change your message every day – at least callers then know that you haven't disappeared for a three month round the world trip. It has the added dimension of making you appear more efficient. If you are going on holiday then different rules apply (see below).

<u>A brief description of your movements</u> – with the emphasis on brief. You are trying to manage expectation. If you are going to be out all day, say so, then people won't be expecting a call back within the hour. If you will be in and out of meetings all day, say so. Callers are then unlikely to keep ringing back to try and get you.

<u>A brief alternative</u> – be careful with this one as it can backfire. If you have a colleague who has agreed to pick up and sort out your calls then leave an alternative extension. Don't leave alternative contact numbers unless you can be sure they will deliver a result. You don't want people chasing round after you and reaching a succession of voicemail systems. If you put your mobile number as an alternative, make sure you are going to be available to answer it.

Voicemail – the 'Dos'

<u>Talk fast</u> – at least faster than normal. This will get the message over quicker and increase the sense of enthusiasm in your voice. A slow dirge of a message will leave people with the impression that you're never very keen about being in work.

<u>Use a standard message</u> – change the details every day, but keep the message in a format that you're used to. This will mean that when you dictate it, it will flow naturally and without interruption.

<u>Speak clearly</u> – pay some attention to your diction, don't run words together or mumble. If you do people will have no idea when you'll call them back and in some instances they may begin to hope you won't bother.

Just before you start your message, inhale deeply. You should be able to dictate the whole thing without breathing in and out again. If not then it's probably too long. This is a good way of keeping the message 'clean'.

<u>Sound bright</u> – plenty of rise and fall in your voice is much better than a dull monotone. Try to picture the caller as someone you like and are genuinely sorry to have missed their call.

<u>Keep your focus</u> – make your message as short and tight as you can, without appearing unfriendly, tell callers what they need to know and finish by promising you will get back to them. Make sure you deliver on this promise as soon as you possibly can.

<u>Always listen back</u> – make sure you haven't clipped the start or end of the message or left too much space before the tone. Few people like the way they sound on voicemail, but try to be objective. If you were a big customer ringing up what impression would the message you've just recorded convey? Is this someone you'd like to do business with? If the answer's no, then re-record it.

The 'Don'ts'

<u>Don't waffle</u> – you are already on the back foot by not being there so it's unlikely the caller will want to hear a long message

about how busy you are and why you can't take the call in person. Be businesslike but friendly.

<u>Don't leave a flawed message</u> – If you get it wrong in any way at all then re-record it. This includes tone of voice, uncertainty about what you're saying, umming and erring or the background noise of colleagues shouting across the office.

<u>Don't try to be funny</u> – Flippant remarks and sarcasm are out. Your immediate peers might find this highly amusing, but it's less likely that one of your customers will! Even if your message is genuinely funny, they won't be laughing at it in 3 months when they've heard it a dozen times.

<u>Don't use someone else to record it</u> – You'll simply look like you don't care who calls you – a personalised message is much better.

<u>Don't use voicemail unless you have to</u> – Switching it on as a way of vetting incoming calls is a really bad idea. Most people will soon work out you're doing this, which means that whenever they hear your voicemail message they'll think that you're available but not willing to speak to them. Apart from anything else, most successful business communication comes from listening and talking so it's plain stupid to try and cut it out.

<u>Don't apologise too much</u> – a lot of grovelling about not being around and how sorry you are that voicemail is the only alternative just wastes more time. Get on with it.

Example 1

A good daily message

'Hi, you're through to Hazel Bloom at The Inn on the Green, on Wednesday November 5th, I'm sorry I'm not around to take your call, you can either leave me a message or try me on my mobile, which is 01234 567 89, that's 01234 567 89. And thanks for your call'.

Example 2

A good holiday message

'Hi you're though to Hazel Bloom at The Inn on the Green. I'm away now until Thursday 20th November, if your call is urgent ring Tricia Hughes on 01234 678 45, that's 01234 678 45, or you can leave me a message and I'll get back to you on my return. And thanks for your call'.

Try this

You can learn a lot from how other people use voicemail.

Make a point of really stopping and listening every time you hear a voicemail message, then answer these three questions.

How well informed am I? Do I think it's worth ringing back? Do I think they'll ring me back? If so, when?

How do I feel? Does the other party come across as keen and enthusiastic? Did it sound as if they cared about missing my call?

What sort of communicator are they, efficient and passionate or lazy and unconcerned?

There are plenty of people who don't like voicemail and won't leave messages, but in these time-pressed days, it is pointless not to use an efficient piece of technology which manages our time and others' expectation.

Pick up your own voicemail regularly and call back as soon as you possibly can. If you encounter other people's voicemail, use it with brevity but in a businesslike way, then you will maximise the potential of the tool.

Outbound calls

We've looked at some methods of dealing with the unpredictability of inbound calls, which should help you take control and manage both your time and the calls themselves more efficiently.

Outbound calls

Although a conversation still ensues with an outbound call, it's different in terms of the level of control you have. Check back with the list of differences at the start of the previous section and you'll see again how outbound calls give you the initiative.

We will deal separately with first-calls, i.e. people you've never spoken to before and then familiar calls, because we need to handle each differently. The latter category could be huge and embrace everything from old friends to a supplier you've dealt with only a few times before, but the same principles should apply.

First-calls

First calls can be critical in establishing the future success, or otherwise of any business relationship, so here are some tips on how to gain and keep the initiative with an initial call.

Before you launch into a monologue about the reason for your call you need to establish that you have reached the right person. That's okay if you've been given the name of an individual to contact, by a reliable source about a specific issue, but if not you need to find out quickly. This might sound obvious, but there are many stories of when 'cold calling' has gone wrong because of a failure to establish who it is we should be talking to. Analyse the purpose of your call and try to sum it up in a single sentence, so whoever you reach will be able to direct you quickly to the right individual.

This is a good discipline for preparing yourself. It isn't difficult if you are calling to book a rail ticket, but if your boss has asked you to find a supplier of high-end graphic design services then you'll need to take more time to prepare.

Once you've made the connection and are talking to the right person you need to check to see how you're getting on in engaging them. This is a skill that will improve with time as long as you stay conscious of the need to do it.

You can use short phrases to check back, like the following examples: 'am I on the right lines here?',' Is this the sort of thing you do?' 'Is this something you think you could help with?'

Even with a first-call, if you engage quickly there can be a mix of social and business chat, just be careful that you don't over play this. You want to appear professional and friendly, but don't overstep the mark when it comes to familiarity, especially with people who are senior in the hierarchy, they tend to be busy and may not be interested in discussing the weekend's football results with you.

Remain businesslike and professional, and don't drag the call out so they feel like they have to get rid of you. Be aware of 'call closing' signals from them and bow out quickly and gracefully. If you get to the stage when they're using the 'anyway' tactic, you've been on too long!

Before your time is up, make provision for summing up the outcome and signposting a way forward. So if one or both of you have agreed to do something, make sure you have covered the ground of when you will next be in contact and by what method. Where circumstances dictate be assertive enough to suggest you call them back and nominate a date and time before asking if that suits them.

You may want to check back one final time, to make sure that they have got what they needed from the conversation.

Those key points again are as follows:

Prepare to an appropriate level

Is this the right person?

Listen for signs of their mood

Check back often

Listen for 'closing' signals

Make a final check back to clarify that a definite outcome has been reached

Familiar calls

The up side of this kind of call is that it is generally much easier to manage; you stand a better chance of being able to govern the length, subject matter and tone of the call with a known person than a stranger. The down side is that over-familiarity can easily creep in, which can result in long rambling chats about anything but the subject in hand. As we say above, it's a question of balancing social and business chat to get the best result in any set of circumstances.

Being too businesslike and never having time for small talk can be quite intimidating, and might leave the other party feeling you lack any kind of empathy. On the contrary, a stream of witless gossip, with no business discussion whatever will make them wonder how you ever get any work done!

Clearly we have to be sensitive to the needs of individuals, some like to exchange pleasantries before getting down to business, others are less inclined to do so, the golden rule here is to listen hard, pick up on the signals and make a mental note of the differences between the personalities you deal with.

It's okay too, to make notes (mental or otherwise) about their interests, the names of their children or other such details, so that you have some common ground in future conversations, but beware of overplaying this or you'll end up looking shallow!

The last thing to remember about outbound calls is that you can use them as a key element of your time management. If you make a prioritised list, you can govern the time of day and duration of many of your outbound calls (if you're not yet in the habit of doing this, then there's some great advice coming up in the next section).

Mostly, you'll be able to govern the time of the call, so try and apply some sensible criteria. Make important calls in the morning when you are most attentive, save routine ones for the afternoon.

If you have to make a lot of calls that require the same output, for example, if you are trying to arrange appointments, then complete them all in one block. This is like applying a production line technique, you begin to get into the swing of it and your efficiency increases.

Use calls that have lighter subject matter (to a close colleague or friend), as a reward, and schedule them in for when you've finished writing that heavyweight report.

Meetings

> *'I think meetings are a good opportunity to listen, but they have to be action orientated too, otherwise they just become talking shops'.*
>
> Chris Major – Astra Zeneca

A staple of the business communication world is the meeting and there is a very good reason for that.

'The most important thing in communication will forever be face-to-face meetings, because it's humanity, not technology that rules. Face-to-face will forever be the most important...why? Because people remember 80% of what they see and only 20% of what they hear and that's fact. So, if you're there talking to them, they remember 4 times more of what you're saying'.

Business meetings have become one of our primary methods of communication and they can take many forms. How useful any individual meeting is will depend on your role, your control and your expectation.

Here are some of the types of meeting you may be involved with.

A regular team briefing to let everyone know about (and discuss), the issues of the day/week.

A one-to-one meeting with your immediate boss to discuss a project you are working on or to set objectives for the coming weeks.

A get together with a customer to discuss the possibility of a new order, or ways of improving service to them.

A brainstorming meeting to generate new ideas to solve problems.

What all these scenarios have in common is that they will run far more smoothly and have much more positive results for you, if time is taken in advance to consider the purpose, method and desired outcome of the meeting. Without this, your meetings will drift on endlessly with no real purpose.

How to prepare for meetings

If you come out of a meeting bored, frustrated or simply angry at the lack of any tangible action then some of it might be down to how well *you* prepared. Equally, it may also be due to the lack of preparation of the other parties to the meeting, but we are not always able to control that, we can however do something about our own input.

It's much more likely that the outcome will be positive if you take just a short time to get yourself together before you enter the fray. Begin by thinking about what the meeting is for. You'd be surprised at the number of people who turn up not knowing and this lack of clarity helps to drag meetings down to the lowest common denominator. When you know the reason for the meeting you can establish your role, and on that basis will be able to make an informed assessment of how much prep time you should put in.

If you look in your diary and see 'Weekly sales performance update', then you might be interested but have little input (other than your listening skills). If, however, it's time for 'Annual performance appraisal', on which your future promotion and financial prospects depend, it might just be worth taking a bit more time out to prepare!

Next consider who the meeting is with. There are two factors to think about, firstly, the *number* of people, and secondly, their *status*. If it's an internal meeting are these people your peers, your staff, the board of management? Knowing who the personnel attending are will also help to inform your preparation.

External meetings might be with customers, suppliers or the general public and will require a different type of preparation. As with most communication issues, the audience is the key.

Answering the question 'who' will point you towards how much control you're likely to have. A client meeting, at their premises, to an agenda that they've drawn up is unlikely to leave you much room for manoeuvre, but at least take the time to read what's going to be discussed so that you have an opinion, or in the worst case scenario, a defence.

According to...

Chris Major – Astra Zeneca

'I used to attend meetings run by a very senior civil servant who would come with the draft minutes already prepared, which was his attempt to be clear about the conclusions he wanted.

With every item he'd just scribble a few changes to the draft that he'd made to capture the discussion that had gone on around the table, and he would actually conclude each item with "well would you all agree that we have decided this?"

Once you knew he was doing it that way my goodness the meetings used to roll along! I wouldn't recommend that for everybody but it is an interesting approach.'

This looks a bit too much like a dictatorship for most modern businesses to contend with, but it does teach us that if you can govern the pace and content of the discussion, you're much more likely to get your own way.

If you're in a meeting where you have only limited control, you'll need to think carefully about the timing of your input. Sometimes it is best to hear what other people think before offering our own opinion. It tells you the lie of the land, the strength of feeling and what objections you might have to overcome.

When it comes to keeping a record of what has been said, this still tends to be in the form of minutes, if your meeting is a formal one. However, in many circumstances, the level of record keeping can be agreed with the other attendees. If you decide there is no need to take detailed minutes, agree with your colleagues what level of 'recording' should take place.

It can be tempting to not bother at all, but the end result is that meetings become much less effective. At the very least you need a list of action points, a name against each and a date by when they must be completed. If you're chairing a meeting it's a good idea to sum up with this list at the end, so that everyone is clear what they have to do before you next get together. Taking responsibility for these action points is often a way of driving what we do on a day-to-day basis, so volunteer your services where appropriate, you don't want to be seen as slow to come forward. In turn, this will allow you to feedback to a future meeting on the level of success you have achieved.

When to contribute

Having done all your preparation for a meeting, it can be tempting to steam in at top speed when your particular agenda items arise. If a controversial topic is up for debate, and you know that others will probably have the opposite viewpoint to you, there are times when it's good to state your case first, particularly if you have a persuasive argument that is hard to counter. But it's often the case that issues are more finely balanced, and in these situations we have already suggested it can be no bad thing to sit back and listen to what others have to say first.

This gives you the opportunity to assess the strength of feeling in the room, to work out who is on which side and who is open to persuasion and it allows you the time to amend your own arguments before you open your mouth.

According to...

> Simon Terrington – Human Capital
>
> 'Be aware of the power of listening. Usually the more senior a person is at a meeting, the less they'll talk and the more they'll listen'.

Really effective persuasion is about weighing all the factors carefully, then constructing your messages in a way that they're likely to gain maximum acceptance. Sometimes it really is only fools who rush in.

Celtic passion

An enthusiastic Welsh manager became well known for his impassioned outbursts during meetings. He would deliver an emotional soliloquy on virtually any subject, often setting himself up as the champion of the underdog. On first seeing this happen his colleagues were awe struck, when he'd finished they broke out into spontaneous applause.

Sadly, further investigation revealed that although the passion burned like an inferno in his very soul, there was little to match it inside his head. In fact, there was rarely, if ever, a logical argument to back what he said and if challenged with 'what practical steps do you think we should take to make things better?" he had to confess that he had no idea!

No one is denying that passion is a powerful weapon in the communicators' armoury, but always remember that substantive argument is a good thing to have too!

How long to prepare?

There's no set of rules that governs how long you spend preparing, it's a question of judgement. What will help to guide you though is expectation. Think about what you want from the meeting and then put yourself in the shoes of the other party.

You might not see a routine meeting with one of your own team as that important, but for them it could be critical. Are they working on a project that's reached a difficult stage? Do they need help with problem solving? Is there friction with other members of the team? These issues may well be unknown to you in advance, but if you are at least aware of how important this get-together is you will be more prepared to listen patiently and work together towards a solution.

Finally, it's always a good idea to check where the meeting is to be held. This is important for the obvious reason that you don't want to turn up at the wrong place!

A Good Story

A junior manager at the BBC had been invited to attend a briefing to be held by the Director General. Although unsure of how she'd ended up on the guest list (most of the other managers due to attend were much more senior), she nevertheless set off in plenty of time.

Arriving at Broadcasting House in central London, she made her way up the main stairwell towards the Boardroom, where she thought the meeting was due to take place. Who should pass her on the way down but the Director General.

'"Excuse me", she said, "but I was coming to your meeting, isn't it in the Boardroom?" Politely he explained that it wasn't even in the same building, but as he was being chauffeured across town to the real venue, perhaps he could offer her a lift.

They arrived at the correct destination to find that the fire alarm had gone off, staff had been evacuated and were standing on the pavement outside. There were some curious glances when the chauffeur opened the door and let out, first the DG and then her!'

Where a meeting is being held can also be a vital part of a successful outcome because the surroundings can change the dynamic of the meeting in a dramatic fashion.

According to…

Professor David Clutterbuck

'Look at the space and environment for your discussion. A practical example was a Chief Executive who I was working with who could not get her top team of managers to be open with her.

She said that communications around the table were difficult. I asked her "which table?" and she said "this one". It was the table in her office. So we asked "what do you think having all the meetings in your office is saying, and how is that affecting the quality of the communications?"

She changed the location and suddenly, Bingo! Everyone started opening up.

How useful was that?'

The point of the story centres around territory. Very often people's surroundings and environment can affect their behaviour, especially when it comes to their willingness to contribute their opinion. In this example, choosing a more neutral venue put people at their ease and they were consequently far more willing to join in.

Post-meeting afterglow

It's tempting after a long meeting to find some means of escape. You might rush back to your workstation and start on the email backlog; alternatively you may head for the canteen for a coffee or out of the back door for a cigarette.

Very few people take the time to think what they've learned from a meeting. If you do take the time to reflect, it is much more likely you will be able to improve the quality of your meetings in future.

When it's all over, ask yourself these questions.

What did I learn?

What did I 'teach'?

What did we decide?

What did we create?

What did we exchange?

The reason for these questions is that they are fundamental to the success of all meetings. Did I hear anything new or tell the rest of the participants something they didn't already know? Collectively did we take any action that will help us, either through reaching an agreement about something or by pooling our collective knowledge and creativity? What it eventually boils down to is what did I take to the meeting and what did I bring back from it? What was the point of it all?

Just a short time reflecting on this will give you an objective picture of whether or not the meeting was useful and that in itself will help you in planning for the next one.

Presentations

Forget all the scare stories about public speaking and pre-sentations; it's really easy when you get the hang of it. That doesn't mean you won't be nervous before the start, but remember that the applause of an appreciative audience is the kind of instant gratification that it's hard to find elsewhere.

If you keep the end point in mind, it will help steer your preparation and give you a much better chance of being a success.

Attention span

They say every time the goldfish swims round the bowl is like a fresh experience; it simply can't remember that it's been there before. There's plenty of evidence to suggest that we are becoming increasingly like the poor goldfish as time goes by! Broadcast media are a great reflection of this. There is an ongoing policy of signposting so that we always know what's coming up next and this is often interspersed with references of what we are currently tuned to, just in case we've forgotten. It is probably linked with the fact we are bombarded by messages all the time and in order to keep our attention, we need reminders on a regular basis. It is as well to remember this when you are presenting and have plenty of signposting in place.

DOGS

Most TV channels now carry digital on screen graphics or DOGS, as a reminder of the station we are tuned to. These normally appear in the corner of the screen, often with a slightly trans-lucent quality so we can see the programme behind them. In a multi-channel environment, each TV network feels the need to remind viewers which station they are tuned to.

We can learn from the world of television when we are called upon to put together a presentation.

When you are faced with keeping your audience engaged there are three principle ways of doing it.

Expectation

Content

Style

Expectation – if you tell your audience up front about what's on the menu then there is a chance they will stay with you, but there's a catch. You have to get content and style right too. So, for example, if you manage their expectation by saying 'For the next hour I am going to explain to you our order processing system in fine detail, using no visual aids, no audience participation and in a dull monotone voice', then you may have told them what to expect but they'll hardly feel engaged. Even with difficult, tedious detail, most audiences will stick with you if you're prepared to explain why and how you intend to present the information.

So, a better start would be

'During the next hour, I need to explain our order processing system so we can open the debate about how to make it better.

I'll start with a quick graphic showing the ten steps of the process, then spend a couple of minutes going through each one. I'll also give you the input of our production team and customer panel at each stage, so you'll get an idea of how well the process serves us and what it delivers, or fails to deliver, to customers'.

The whole issue of managing expectation is vital if you are to succeed.

According to...

Alistair Smith – Alite

'Draw attention throughout to what it is you're doing and explain not only the content but your thinking behind it. Keep the audience focussed on the content and don't present yourself as an authority figure. A lot of people make that mistake "listen to me because I'm an expert", but then you're into a dog fight, it's a challenge to prove you are as good as you say you are'.

Professor David Clutterbuck gives his thoughts on what contributes towards a successful presentation.

The Expert Panel

Professor David Clutterbuck

'The first thing is not to get in the way of the message. One of the first lessons I was taught was to look at how you dress and not to wear bright coloured socks for example because they distract people, not to have too many slides because again it distracts people from the message.

Make it easy for people to listen to you and that means not standing behind a podium unless you can help it. Get out among them and always think about it as a conversation.

If I think about giving a lecture it always gets stilted, if I think about having a conversation with people then it's much easier and that doesn't matter if I'm with a thousand people or four people.

That means I spend a lot of time listening to them as well, you really need to interact with your audience from the very first point.

The amount of information they absorb is much higher if they've had some engagement in its construction, so instead of putting up a load of slides and reading them out, I would get them to talk about what's on the slides.

Often you'll know what an audience wants to hear but if you engage them then they'll tell you. There's no argument about it then'.

Professor David Clutterbuck is a well established and extremely competent speaker. By his own admission much of this has come about because he has worked hard on his technique.

Live presentations are one of the most difficult aspects of communication to master. All the advice in the world will only take us so far, the critical element is practice, the more you do, the better you get.

Managing PowerPoint

Because it is so widely used in presentations, we think it is necessary to devote some time to the use of PowerPoint as an aid to presentation. We have already said that before you've even put up your first slide, it's a good idea to manage the expectation of your audience. Often professional presenters use a 'holding slide' one that simply has the title of their presentation on. This allows them to signpost their content, before getting into the detail of the first slide.

If you have a small number of slides, say so at the start.

'I just want to run you through a short PowerPoint presentation to illustrate my case, it's actually only half a dozen slides and it'll take about 15 minutes'.

It can be a good idea if you have a medium number of slides to put the number on each, so as the slide comes up it'll say 'number 1 of 20' and so on, giving the audience the chance to assess how long is left.

If you have a large number of slides then break it down into more manageable pieces. Again it helps if you are up front.

'Okay, there are about 60 slides to go through but they're in 3 distinct sections, as follows, "where are we now?, where do we want to be?, and how do we get there?" (This ties in with our advice on lists of three).

We'll just be spending ten minutes on each section as there are quite a lot of graphs and illustrations and that should leave us enough time to debate the issues that arise'.

This is a good start to a PowerPoint presentation, but you also have to remember to use the tool in the right way. Technique is all important.

According to...

Professor Cary Cooper

'What is really bad, from a communication point of view, is when someone puts a PowerPoint presentation up and reads each of the 12 things on each of the 12 slides in slow time. I just flash the slide up and pick out a couple of points then move on, I think you shouldn't leave any slide up for more than 45 seconds.

I'd also avoid doing numbered lists because people are waiting for the next point, it's much better if it's non-linear because you then have the flexibility to make the points you want without being tied into some kind of chronology that doesn't work'.

As with all technology there are risks that the equipment will let you down and sometimes this can happen at the most critical point of your address. It's a good idea to have a contingency plan if you can.

According to...

Simon Terrington – Human Capital

'When I do a big presentation I have paper prints of the slides and distribute them to the audience, so if it crashes you can just say, "turn to page 6 on the document in front of you" and you can keep going. Of course you can only do that with 20 people, you can't do it with 200'.

Under some circumstances it is best not to give out a hard copy at the start of the presentation though, as people will tend to skip ahead rather than listen to what you're saying. In the case of a sales pitch, the greatest likelihood is that they'll be on the last page (where the pricing information usually appears), before you're halfway through the first slide.

Top tips for using PowerPoint effectively

Try to keep the number of slides as few as possible, remember they are a bulleted form of your presentation, not the whole thing!

Manage your audience's expectation, let them know how many slides you're using right at the start.

Keep text simple, don't clutter your slides with too many bullet points and never use blocks of text.

Think of slides like poster advertisements, use the same amount of information you would fit on a hoarding and your slides will work really well.

Use pictures; graphic illustrations can make a point better than words.

Keep it pacey, don't leave one slide up for too long. Remember the 45 second rule.

In this chapter, we've dealt with many of the most commonly used tools of communication. All of these technologies were developed to help us make our daily interaction more effective, but it's easy for the opposite to apply, if the tools are used badly.

The Elevator Test for Chapter 10

- Listening and talking are vital components of good relationships – they are at the core of communication

- Apply strict criteria to incoming phone calls to assess how vital they are to your working day and then manage them appropriately

- Manage your outbound calls and plan them effectively. Don't snatch up the handset and dial without thinking

- Pay special attention to 'first calls, they're the starting point for new relationships'

■ How productive meetings are is often governed by your role, your control and your expectation

■ Not all meetings are of equal importance, allocate your planning time accordingly

■ If you're presenting to an audience, engage them with expectation, content and style

■ PowerPoint is immensely powerful – in the right hands!

CHAPTER 11

Feeling

Non-verbal communication

Introduction

If it really were true that what you see is what you get we wouldn't need to consider the importance of body language. But because we are human and complex, there are many non-verbal signals we transmit and receive all the time, all of which contribute to the deeper understanding of the messages that are passed between us.

In truth, we don't always say what we mean. In the forming of any new relationship, whether business or personal, there is much left unsaid and it is often the silent signals we send which are the most telling.

We're going to take a look at some of the most common forms of non-verbal communication and try to understand what the signals mean, so we can better manage what we're transmitting through our actions and understand more of what other people are 'saying' to us through their deeds rather than their words.

First impressions

Sir John Hall, the businessman behind The Metro Centre and Newcastle Football Club was asked by a conference delegate, how long it took him to assess a company he was dealing with when he visited their premises.

'A matter of seconds' was his typically blunt reply.

His view is further supported by one of our panel of experts.

According to...

Professor Chris Brewster

'The research tells us quite clearly that people form an impression literally within about 20 seconds, and there is very little you can do afterwards to change that impression. You fight it from then on, or reinforce it.

I think a lot of communicators don't think seriously enough about that, so they start their conversation with "ah, well, errm, like errm, sort of err, it's nice to be here" sort of thing and if that's the first impression people get then it really is bad news. So I really believe that first impressions are one of the key moments of truth'.

We cannot help ourselves making snap judgements when we encounter other individuals for the first time. There are times when our initial instincts about them are wrong, but more often than not we are correct, based on a mixture of experience and intuition.

But if we are doing this to other people, we can be sure they are making the same judgements about us. So what can we do to make the best first impression?

Preparation and planning is essential when you're out to make a positive impact. To do your current job you probably had to go through some sort of selection interview, so you should have considered many of these things already.

Appearance

We may like to think it is our substance which is more important than our style, but the harsh reality is that appearances count. You don't have to dress in Armani, but you do have to look like you've made the effort. Have your best shoes seen better days? Does your suit look like a throwback to a previous decade? If so, it's time to smarten up.

If you are not sure how to present yourself, ask the advice of someone you trust. It's important to remember that you are presenting a first impression of you, not a catalogue model or a shop dummy, so choose clothes you feel comfortable in. When you are happy with the way you look it's far more likely you'll relax quickly and be yourself and that helps you to show your best side.

When you look in the mirror, try to see yourself from someone else's point of view, don't go against type and try shock tactics with a bright flowery dress or a big hat unless you'd dress like that anyway. Even if you do, remember that most people prefer surprises to shocks, so tone it down a bit until they've got to know you better.

The golden rule of comfort is to tick both boxes, physically in terms of the fit of your clothes and emotionally with regard to how you feel about yourself, when you're dressed this way.

Personal grooming is important too, pay attention to staying neat and tidy. Clean hair and nails are a must.

With things like make up and perfume or after shave, subtlety is the key, avoid anything too imposing.

How do I look?

In the hyper-competitive eighties, the photocopying business was as ruthless as any. The organisations at the top of the pile were typified by a macho culture, where communication was very direct and the 'will to win' extremely strong.

Under these circumstances virtually anything could be seen as an area of competitive advantage over other players in the market. At the foot of the stairs, of a regional office of the leading manufacturer was a full-length mirror, which no sales person could avoid seeing on their way out. Above it was printed, 'Would you buy from this man?'

A Good Story

How do I look too?

A spiteful press will always try to find ways of criticising a politician whose views they don't share. In Liverpool in the

1980s, one such leading figure was Derek Hatton. Not content with disagreeing with his political views, some papers sought to undermine him by criticising his fastidious personal grooming and taste in clothes, which included expensive suits. At the time they printed a story saying that the mirror in Hatton's office bore the legend, 'Yes Derek, you do look brilliant!'

Behaviour

Be yourself
At least be the most universally acceptable version of yourself under the circumstances. That means until you've had the opportunity to find your feet and understand a little better what the other party is looking for. Err on the side of caution to begin with. If you get past first base there will be plenty of time to assert the true you. Over familiarity too soon can be very threatening.

According to...

Simon Terrington – Human Capital

'There's some interesting work been done on intimacy which is that if I meet you for the first time and I hardly know you, and we're having a chat, and I say, "by the way I've got an embarrassing disease", you'd be absolutely shocked because I've jumped to a level of intimacy you just don't want to be at.

Whereas if we start off slowly and we become friends and I say in a spirit of confidentiality and concern that I've got it, then it's something you can deal with and support me. But to get to those levels of intimacy people have to offer the same back until you go deeper and deeper. It has to be a balance'.

It's also true that if you consciously want to get closer to someone, a starting point is to reveal something personal about yourself. Under normal circumstances, this will lead them to trade a similar piece of information in return and the process continues with the result you get to know each other better and better.

Body language

Body language is an important part of communication, but it has been so over analysed as a subject it has begun to become a bit of a cliché.

When it first came to prominence we were told it was a way of sending out subliminal messages to other people while simultaneously being able to read them with a greater degree of accuracy. It may be in some cases this is true, but we are keen not to overplay this aspect of communication.

As part of our communications tool box we need to be aware of body language and its significance. We have covered some of these aspects when looking at 'active listening' but it is worth consolidating them now.

We need to have an understanding what different signs mean and where possible we should be sensitive to the signals the other party is sending out, but the likelihood is we are already well tuned to pick up these unconscious signals.

As far as controlling our own body language in order to send out only the signals we choose there is a limit to what we can do. In a stress or conflict situation, for example, we are more likely to adopt a closed, defensive position and making a conscious effort to change our posture is only likely to last for a short time before we revert to type again. It takes a lot of practice and concentration to override our bodies' natural tendencies.

A better solution is to concentrate on the root cause of our body language, by tracing the way we are behaving back to its source. Once we learn to manage our feelings, our body language will fall into line behind.

According to...

Alistair Smith – Alite

'You've only got the one body and you've developed a set of mannerisms, a way of walking, a way of standing that all your life has been invested in, so it's difficult to undo that.

There are certain superficial things that you can alter and undo, so if when you're doing a presentation and you jangle the change in your pocket because you're nervous, take it out before you start and the problem is half way to being solved.

But overall the theory that body follows mind holds true, so what you tend to get is non-verbal leakage.

What that means is that if mentally you're in anguish then physiologically your body reflects that in high anxiety, you literally leak, you perspire. In fact that's how lie detectors work!'

The key elements of body language

Here are some simple things you can look out for to give you clues about the way people are feeling.

<u>Eye contact</u> – often described as the window to the soul, the eyes can give away a lot about what the other party is thinking. Sometimes though, the signs can be open to misinterpretation. Eye contact can signal attraction, or it can be very threatening. For that reason you have to read it along with other things, like tone of voice or stance.

If someone makes sustained eye contact with you over a candlelit dinner that is one thing, it is entirely different from the eye contact from a mugger in the street who is demanding money with menace. You don't need to be an expert in human behaviour to work that out.

<u>Body posture</u> – a closed position might be sitting hunched with arms folded and legs crossed and it naturally looks defensive. However, this could be caused by a whole series of circum-stances, maybe guilt over having not done something, simply being nervous in the present company or possibly secretive about sensitive information. They all look the same, but may require different approaches to get the other party to relax.

The contrary open position, feet apart, arms loosely at sides, sitting upright, suggests the very opposite. This is someone who's in control of the situation and relaxed about it. They're far more likely to be ready to indulge in an open exchange of views.

<u>Mirroring</u> – this is the behaviour people undertake when they want the other party to like them. It is most stark when observed amongst courting couples. In an attempt to show approval for the other person we match our gestures and movements to theirs. As one party picks up their drink, so the other follows a fraction of a second later. What we can learn from this is that if someone is mirroring us, they like us, which is useful when trying to get our message across.

According to...

Simon Terrington – Human Capital

'Mirroring is really interesting and if you analyse good sales people they really mirror the blinking and the facial twitches and all the actions of the person they're talking to and they have this incredible ability that is totally to do with empathy'.

On the other hand a complete lack of empathy can lead to the breakdown of a relationship. This can be very stressful and once again body language can leak emotions. Harsh exchanges of words can be accompanied by non-verbal communication that's equally challenging.

John Akers has been mediating between couples for many years, often bringing both parties together in the same room for the first time since the split. This is the sort of thing he has witnessed.

The Expert Panel

John Akers
Relationship Counsellor

'I see a range of facial expressions. Other important non-verbal cues are chair positioning, playing with your hands, not having eye contact or alternatively having quite fierce eye contact, being intent on writing notes this sort of thing.

You see cases of people trying to avoid engaging personally either with the mediator or the ex-partner, or even the opposite, trying to woo the mediator onto their side and some women can be very adept at that and use their sexual powers to what they hope will be great advantage.

The smiles and the leg crossing I think may not be entirely unintentional'.

Try this

Take half an hour out to do some people watching. Find a busy coffee bar in town and note down what you observe.

What first impression do people make on you, is that altered when you hear them speak or see what they order?

Watch out for people meeting up, how do they greet each other, what does it tell you about each of them, about their relationship? By their body language do they look like friends or work colleagues, what is the balance of power between them?

Look around. Who seems relaxed and comfortable, who looks tense or stressed? What do you think might be causing it? This is a great way of coming to understand the finer points of non-verbal communication and makes you think much harder about the effects your actions have on others, before you've even uttered a word.

Touching

> *'Some cultures like touching, in southern Europe to hold someone by the arm just shows you're engaging with them, whereas if you're in Scandinavia that might be seen as being close to an assault'.*
>
> Professor Chris Brewster

An important issue related to body language is touching. We're not talking about full-on hugging, just a light gesture like a hand in the small of the back as you go through into a meeting, or the leaning across and squeezing of a forearm to show a connection.

As Professor Chris Brewster points out in his opening remarks, the problem with touching is that it can be very open to mis-interpretation. It is something that doesn't work well across cultures.

According to...

Simon Armson – The Samaritans

'The other thing you have to take account of is culture, the British are fairly undemonstrative, but some of the Latin races are far more likely to touch.

It can be a good thing to confirm something that's important.

The communication that comes from physical touching need not to be totally excluded, but it has to be carefully put into context in terms of appropriateness'.

Even within a single culture our upbringing, social class and environment can have a profound effect on our willingness to touch or be touched. Some men may feel uncomfortable being touched by women in case they wrongly interpret it as a sign of attraction. In some circumstances men feel uneasy about being touched by other men, for fear of being seen as less macho.

Women may feel threatened by a man who is a frequent toucher, even if he appears not to be interested in them in other ways.

Fathers and sons often find it hard to touch or embrace, particularly during the 'teenage' years.

Teams involved in sport may find it easier to touch than other groups (they are usually well used to embracing after a goal has been scored!)

According to…

John Akers – Relationship Counsellor

'I think its now more acceptable for a man to hug his son than it ever was and I think that's a good thing. Certainly I hug my own son, but I can't remember my father hugging me. I just think that's because things have changed.

In the jargon you'd say that men are now a little more aware of their feminine side, which is a phrase that's always amused me because I don't see why it's a particularly feminine thing to touch'.

Certainly within British culture it does look as though attitudes are changing, though we still have to be careful of the circumstances under which we consider touching as it can mean different things at different times.

According to…

Simon Armson – The Samaritans

'It can mean all sorts of things and it depends entirely on the circumstances and the environment and the expectations and so on of the people concerned. It can be threatening it can also be enabling, it can be supportive, it can be empathetic it can communicate a degree of closeness that words wouldn't reach'.

Culture

> *'Culture is how people behave when they're not thinking about it'.*
> Michael Angus – Former Chairman of Unilever

Culture has already come up, but why is it so important?

What we're trying to do is assess and monitor the effect of our surroundings on the way we communicate, because it's only if you can set your messages into some kind of relevant context that you'll stand any chance of them being well received.

There are two types of culture that we're going to look at here; one is the difference between nations, the other centred on organisations.

You may not have reached a stage in your career where you're hopping on and off planes as you sort out your company's problems around the world, but with the increasing global nature of business and the our increasingly mixed race communities, we all now need to be aware of how to cope with different cultures. Here are some tips on how to avoid getting it wrong.

<u>Read up</u> – if you know that you are going to be handling all incoming calls from your organisation's office in Delhi, then either go to the library and get an appropriate book or do some online research that tells you about lifestyle, religion, custom and practice and even social norms.

<u>When in Rome</u> – try to adapt yourself to the other culture instead of expecting them to adapt to you. If you end up working in a multi-cultural environment, (which is more and more likely these days), then be prepared to give ground and you'll soon find that people will respond, allowing you to find a compromise that suits both cultures.

According to…

> Surinder Hundal – Nokia
>
> 'When I took my first trip to China I was only there for a week, during which I did 3 days of sightseeing and then 2 days of business because that is what I was expected to do. I was expected to know the country and the people before I sat down and engaged with them.
>
> There's not a hope in hell of me doing that in Finland, it's like, "come in and get stuck into business right away", so you have to pay attention to that kind of thing'.

<u>Be polite</u> – We doubt that there's any nation that is deliberately rude, but certainly in business some countries take a much more direct and focussed approach than others and have little time for small talk. For the time being, it's much better to err on the side of courtesy, at least until you've come to terms with the work ethic of the other party.

<u>Ask for feedback</u> – if you think you may have overstepped the mark or caused offence, then politely ask if this is the case and apologise for your cultural ignorance. Most people will forgive most things if they believe it's a genuine mistake, but consistently serving bacon sandwiches when the Rabbi visits isn't likely to win you any friends in the Synagogue!

According to…

> Lynn Rutter – Oxfam
>
> 'Once, when I was in a hotel in Kuala Lumpur I rang down and ordered "a table for 7 o'clock please for room 327" and they said, "would you like a chair as well?" and I said, "of course thank you" and was quite huffy that they were "taking the Mickey".
>
> But lo and behold at 7 o'clock, as I'm just about to leave my room, there's a knock on the door and in they came with a table and chair, which they put down, bowed politely and went out, no doubt thinking "stupid foreigner" and I'd

been thinking "stupid foreigner", but it's an example that emphasised my own cultural arrogance.

Of course I then had to ring down for room service!'.

As well as the obvious point that Lynn Rutter makes about cultural differences, there's an important lesson here too about the need for clarity in all the communications we make.

The Expert Panel

Lynn Rutter
Oxfam

'I didn't go to university and my first job was working as a tea trolley lady at Green Shield Stamps. It formed my communications skills in a great way, because I was working alongside glorious people like Annie and Flo and Gladys, who were the salt of the earth trolley ladies and I didn't want to come across as some stuck up middle class kid.

So you learn very fast to listen to people and pick up on what they're saying and communicate at the various levels that they need you to communicate at.

I don't mean that in any way these people were not bright, but they didn't have an academic vocabulary so there was no point in talking on a high foluting level. You had to talk to people about what you wanted them to do in a very straightforward and simple and plain and understandable way and I guess that was a very good lesson.

You saw a lot of the office workers treating these people like they were dirt because they hadn't got a degree and they didn't go to the right school and they hadn't done the correct things and actually these people were far more passionate about what they did than the stuck-up office workers.

So you learned very quickly that you have to adapt your style of communication, not expect them to adapt their level of understanding'.

Watch and listen – rather than charging headlong into your new relationship, be a little more reserved and take the time to watch and listen. This is all the more valuable if you are alongside a colleague from the same background as yourself, who has had some experience of the culture you are integrating into.

More and more companies are coming across the challenges of managing and communicating across different cultures, as society in general becomes more multi racial, and bigger organisations operate in many markets. Here we've talked about some of the subtleties of different cultures, but it's also worth noting that some things cut across all boundaries, fundamentals like respect, openness and courtesy are never out of place.

According to…

Bill Dalton – HSBC

'There are interesting cultural issues in managing global organisations; our experience is that while the cultures may vary, the people aren't that different. Bad communication is bad communication whether it's in the UK, in Canada, in the States, in France, in Asia, Brazil, it's no different. So the rules that apply in many cases apply because communication by definition involves people.

They may have cultural differences, they may use chop sticks instead of knives and forks, but they're going to be just as annoyed if they hear about their boss leaving on an email rather than someone having the common courtesy and respect to come down and tell them before they heard it like everybody else'.

Sometimes, as in some of the examples we've already seen, it is the pace at which business is done, which is one of the primary differences in national cultures.

According to…

Kevin Roberts – Saatchi and Saatchi

'I think the difference is not technology, the difference is attitude, in the UK it's sort of not whether you win or lose but how you place the blame that still matters, people are still doing that. A lot of the communication in the UK is about analysis, excuses, reasons and blaming in corporate life, whereas in the US, it's oh yeah we messed that up, let's move on and get this done now'.

Organisational culture

One of the most powerful drivers of behaviour in organisations is their culture. It is only relatively recently that we have recognised it's significance, as we have become more introspective and analytical about our working lives.

As with many aspects of organisational life, it has both good and bad aspects, so here is a summary of both sides.

Plus

Fosters greater understanding
Keeps us more in touch
We are better able to predict outcomes
Our planning improves
We have a clearer direction

Minus

We become self obsessed
It wastes time
The effect stifles creativity
We are disempowered
Complacency sets in

So on the up side, when we know what makes the organisation tick, we're better able to cope with the ups and downs of corporate life, we have a greater understanding of where we sit versus our competitors (presumably we've spent some time thinking about their culture too), and knowing ourselves makes us better able to perpetuate our culture going forward. This can be helpful if you think about things like recruitment. If you know the nebulous unspoken things that make the company the way it is, it becomes much easier to spot who will be able to adapt to the culture and who won't.

The opposite of all this results in an organisation that is strangled by its own self belief, that it is right in the face of evidence to the contrary. In recent years, we have seen examples of large companies, formerly at the top of their industry, fall from grace, for the simple reason that they convinced themselves that they had all the answers.

When it comes to the kind of blind faith that some organisational cultures perpetuate, it ends with new ideas being squashed and creativity stifled. People simply stop questioning the system.

See if the following anecdote makes you think of an organisation you've worked for.

A Good Story

You take a cage and put five monkeys in it, then at one end of the cage you put a banana. Naturally the monkeys will run to the banana, but when they do you spray them with very cold water. Soon the monkeys learn not to run to the banana.

Then you replace one of the monkeys with a new monkey. When he gets in the cage he looks at the banana, then at the other four dumb monkeys and decides he'll run to the banana.

As he does so, all the other monkeys jump on him and beat him up because they don't want him to suffer like they did and get sprayed with cold water. Effectively they've learned that the banana is out of bounds.

Over time you keep on replacing the old monkeys with new ones, until you have five brand new ones who've never been sprayed with water. You ask any of those monkeys why they don't go to the banana and they will say, 'I don't know, it's just the way we do things around here'.

The awful thing for many organisations is that having done all this navel gazing, they come to the conclusion that there are lots of things about themselves that they don't like and embark on a process of culture change. Be warned, it's a long and difficult process and the changes that happen tend to be only ever incremental.

Whatever the good and bad of all this, if you work for a big organisation you'll be able to think of people who are counter-cultural. Either they're too aggressive in an over-polite culture, or they're not tough enough for an in-your-face culture. Inevitably what happens is that the culture wins and the individuals either adapt or leave, sad in some cases, but it's a fact of life.

When organisational cultures clash there may be a need to find a creative solution to the problem.

The Expert Panel

Professor Chris Brewster

'There's a great story of when IBM took over Lotus Notes. There was a real clash of cultures because Lotus Notes was a pretty wild and creative place, where people would turn up in shorts and t-shirts when they felt like it and, in some cases, the guys even wore dresses, but as long as they were creating new and innovative packages no one really cared.

They got taken over by IBM, which is quite the opposite and the guy from IBM stood up in front of all the people at Lotus and said how wonderful it was that they'd joined together and blah, blah, blah and someone in the audience said "we've got a free and easy culture here and would you ever consider coming to work in a dress?"

And his reply was "You hit the profit target I'm looking for and I'll come to work in a dress", which focussed them on the financial bit that under normal circumstances they'd rather leave to someone else.

For the IBM guy it was clever because he wanted them to concentrate on the profit while at the same time making sure he didn't stifle their culture'.

Case study

A comparison of cultures

Kay Winsper, from Microsoft highlighted corporate cultures by contrasting the differences between her own organisation and the *Financial Times* newspaper. What do you think would be the differences in communication style within the two organisations?

'I did a job swap with Lucy Kellaway a renowned journalist on the F.T.

The main differences in culture between Microsoft and the F.T. were that Microsoft concentrates on teams, but the F.T. is built on individuals and the reward and recognition of individuals. They work on adrenaline on the deadlines, they don't have any processes in place at all other than a 10:30 a.m. meeting to decide the stories, the 11:30 a.m. meeting to decide the headlines. Then you research till 4:30 p.m. and write the article with a 5:30 p.m. deadline.

Any of the journalists I met certainly didn't think about what the future holds; they're not concentrating on next week's article, it's very much about the now.

In terms of the environment, there was a wealth of information on everyone's desk, they were piled high, 4 deep, the only thing that you could see was the keyboard and even around their desks it was just extremely cluttered, but the clutter mattered. It was a totally different environment to Microsoft, but it works for them because you don't see the F.T. with blank pages the next day'.

Our lesson is to not worry unduly about how you adapt your communication within your own organisation because once you've worked there for a few weeks the culture will most likely be oozing out of your pores. You will know where the boundaries are and will not make the mistake of crossing them. What you have to be careful of, is to assume that other organisations have the same culture as yours.

A Good Story

Pretty young things

Part of the tendering process for a major public sector catering contract involved potential suppliers doing a presentation about how they would handle day-to-day situations. A senior figure asked the following of one of the applicants.

'An overseas investor is visiting our office to see about setting up a new factory in the area, which is important for our economic development. I ring you to say we would like lunch laid on, what questions do you ask me?'

The caterer's reply started well. 'I'd ask what stage of the negotiation you were at and what you hoped to achieve from the day, then I'd suggest some way of having a theme at lunchtime that would help make the day memorable for your guests.

So, if it was a formal sit down meal we may supply a couple of waiters dressed as butlers'.

To this point, the answer was excellent, but the presenter had failed to realise the culture of equality and political correctness of the public sector. He buried his chances with the words…

'On the other hand if it was less formal, maybe we'd have couple of pretty young waitresses in short skirts'.

We're not passing judgement on whether he was right or wrong to say this, simply that his mistake was a failure to understand the culture of the organisation he was hoping to win a contract from.

Try this

If you want to improve your empathy skill, that's to say your ability to see the world through other people's eyes, then take the time to step outside yourself by exploring other interests.

A very simple way to achieve this is to buy one magazine a month that you would normally never think of, so if you're a man choose a women's fashion magazine and vice versa. Alternatively you could pick something that is outside your age range, or a specialist interest publication, (photography, flower arranging, showbiz gossip etc.).

Take note of the articles and the advertisements to get a feel for how the average reader of this magazine sees life and don't forget to check out the letters page, for even greater insight.

Not only will you get a view on how other people think, but your speed of intuition will increase too.

The Elevator Test for Chapter 10

- You only have a few seconds to make a first impression

- Clothes, grooming and cosmetics are all important factors

- Act naturally; it's you they want to see

- Your own non-verbal output is hard to control

- Learn to read the basics of eye contact, posture and mirroring

- Touching is risky but significant

- Make the effort to understand the cultures of different nations

- Knowing company culture can help with understanding but stifle creativity

- Be sensitive to the culture of other organisations you deal with

Planning for Success

Some strategies for turning your intentions into actions

CHAPTER 12

Planning

Preparing your personal communication plan

> *'You have to remember that no organisation stands still, so if you don't continually improve your own communication style, by default you will be moving backwards relative to that organisation'.*
>
> Russell Grossman – BBC

Your personal communication strategy will need to be planned too if you are going to get any better. This is where most people begin to switch off as planning has a reputation for being tiresome and boring. Aware of its bad press, we've come up with a quick and simple planning method, which will minimise the time you spend on it, but still maximise the benefit it produces.

Why plan?

Most of the time we are living our lives *unconsciously*. That's to say we wake each morning and perform a routine of tasks; some domestic, some social, some work related and then we go to bed and start the cycle again.

Now and again, we snap out of this state to do an 'occasional' activity, like book a holiday or enjoy the Christmas break, but the older we get, the more times we've performed this task and it too becomes part of the cycle of routine, it just happens less often than brushing our teeth.

How often do you make enough time to sit down and really look at what's going on around you, to think about who you are and whether you're reaching your potential?

Becoming conscious is the first step to breaking the routine and changing the status quo, only then can you start to take decisions about where you're going.

According to...

Jan Shawe – Sainsbury's

'I think people who've been around for a long time know how important it is to make conscious efforts to improve their communication but I think even then you have got to sort of almost diarise it, "when was the last time I spoke to the team etc.?"

At the beginning of the year I'll put in the diary that I want a weekly meeting with my senior team just to make sure it really happens. Whilst it's an instinctive thing to do, I still think it takes a bit of prior planning to make sure those dates and times are put in the diary and are sacred, because it's so easy to cancel things. So there's quite a lot of instinct there but then there's some actual nitty gritty basic action of getting it in the diary and making sure it happens'.

When you've finished planning and started to implement your new strategy you'll find you have so much more time for the things that matter. There's one law of physics that none of us can change, time is finite.

A Good Story

Joe's story

Back in the 1970s, before the days of sophisticated computer technology, most analysis in business had to be done in a painstaking way.

If, for the sake of argument, you wanted to know how many of your customers spent more than £100,000 a year with you, probably the best you could do would be to print out on massive sheets of interlinked computer pages (known as music paper), all the customer names and their expenditure to date.

Joe had the job of going through line-by-line, picking out the names of the big spenders and writing them down on a separate sheet of paper. As the thirst for knowledge increased (it's the only way to stay ahead of the competition), Joe was asked to complete these tasks more and more frequently, until it became almost his whole job.

One day, a naive young subordinate of Joe asked 'Don't you get fed up each time the boss asks you to do another one of these exercises?' to which Joe replied 'Well, if I wasn't doing this, I'd be doing something else'.

That piece of distorted philosophy kept Joe going through the most tedious of tasks, but what it reinforces is the message that time is finite, and because of that it's a valuable resource that we should allocate with thought and care.

This is all the more relevant when you consider the information overload we all suffer from now. We simply have to be more selective about our communication inputs and outputs.

Why we fail

The big mistake we often make (and it causes us to fail), is that we embark on a programme of personal change management that's simply unachievable, over ambitious or plain daft.

Self-improvement – January Gym Syndrome

There's no business more seasonal than the fitness industry.

Estimates suggest that up to 60% of new memberships are signed in the first two weeks of every year, brought about partly by our guilt feelings related to over-indulgence and partly because of the opportunity a new year presents for a fresh start.

Sadly this doesn't last. Statistically you are only likely to attend the gym 12 times before you let your membership lapse.

Take out the visit for your assessment, the couple of times you just used the pool or sauna, the occasion when you'd for-gotten your trainers and the times you couldn't run because you'd pulled a calf muscle and let's face it you've barely burned off the calories of a roast potato.

Failure in most cases results from a combination of over adventurous expectation and the complete absence of a plan.

Rather than re-inventing ourselves, we should be thinking in terms of a plan to make the best of who we are. Although the changes we make will be incremental rather than seismic, having a realistic view of what can be achieved might eventually end with some satisfaction rather than disappointment.

Getting started

Three steps to successful planning

Get conscious
Plan to plan
Tick the box of achievement

You need to be in the frame of mind to change the way things are currently, then you have to make the effort to set some time aside and when it's in your diary you can cross that off your things to do list.

The key to planning successfully is to view it like removing a sticking plaster, peeling slowly doesn't reduce the pain; it just draws it out over a longer period. Take the short, sharp, shock approach and it may hurt like mad at first but it's soon over.

Planning starts here

Take an hour to complete this stage.

What you are aiming to do would take most organisations several days, but you simply don't have that amount of time to waste.

Because of this you will need to focus on the task in hand without any distractions. Choose somewhere quiet, switch phones to voicemail, turn off the computer, make sure you're fed and watered.

It is now vitally important for you to check your watch – you must take no more and no less than an hour for this task.

There are five stages to complete including time for a short review at the end of the hour. Dividing the time up in advance is a good discipline and helps you to keep focussed on the particular task you are working on.

The planning stages are as follows:

Audit

Make time

Target – macro planning & micro planning

Resourcing

Assessment

And they fit into your planning hour like this

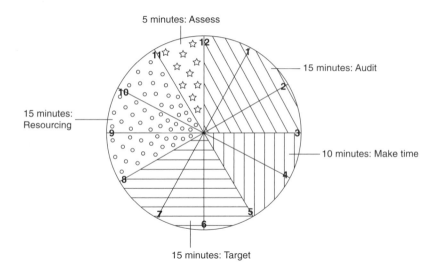

The stages of planning

Audit

This is the phase that answers the question 'where am I now?'

There will be a gap between where you are and where you want to be, so this exercise is about identifying the ways that can be bridged.

You need to work out your **feelings** and your **actions**.

We'll take it as read there are some aspects of your communication you are already fairly happy with. However as we're trying to address the negatives it inevitably means you have to face up to some of the things that currently need more attention.

Try to come up with three statements that sum up how you feel about some of the weaker parts of your personal communication profile.

Here are a few examples to show what we mean.

'I sometimes come out of meetings feeling as though I didn't really have my say'.

'I seem to spend half of my day reading email attachments'.

'I can't seem to conquer my public speaking nerves'.

It's most likely that the issues which are most important to you will surface and that in itself is a good measure of what you'd like to address.

Being aware of your feelings is part of the process, but to stop it getting too unfocussed you also need to look at the practical issues of how you spend your communications time.

Planning audit checklist

How many meetings do you attend each day/week?
What is the average duration of meetings?
What percentage of meetings take more than an hour?
What percentage of meetings overrun?

How many emails do you receive per day/week?
How often do you deal with email (once a day, hourly, when it arrives?)
What percentage of emails are action orientated vs. information giving?
What percentage of incoming emails is badly targeted/not relevant to you?
How often do you send email (once a day, hourly, respond immediately?)

How many presentations (to more than six people), do you do?
What level of preparation do you make?
How many other people are available to help you prepare?

How much time do you spend on the phone each day?

What's the average call duration?

How many calls are vital?

Do you set aside a time of day for outgoing calls or do them as needed?

Conclusion

Most definitely the conclusion you will have come to is that you are wasting too much time on things that aren't important. This is why we continually recommend the need to raise your level of consciousness so that you can really begin to think about what you do each day and make more deliberate choices, rather than becoming part of someone else's agenda, all the while responding, instead of being proactive. The exercise has the added benefit of starting to focus your mind on just which meetings are pointless, which emails irrelevant and phone calls unnecessary.

The trouble with meetings

Every meeting you have has a start time, but rarely, if ever, do they have an end time (unless everyone is booked to go to another meeting later that day!).

We know that work expands to fill the time, but if we were to reverse things and treat the time as the important thing and not the work, the miraculous result is we would find huge chunks of it were now free to do other stuff.

A meeting with no end time results in it meandering this way and that, drifting off at pointless tangents and not always finding its way back to the original purpose. Our minds mirror this journey resulting in concentration lapsing and decision-making becoming difficult if not impossible.

If at the start of the meeting you were to say 'Okay we have half an hour to decide the best way of winning a new order from our biggest customer', you would be sure to stay focussed and come up with more creative answers.

Tough decisions

You need to complete three steps to make more time.

First of all you have to start to ask questions about all of those daily requests that put a call upon your time and come up with hard, objective reasons for allocating it to them. You have to decide on the difference between essential communication and nice-to-have.

Ask yourself some of these questions:

What do I get out of this meeting? What do others get from my being there?

How much of the email that I receive is relevant? How much is personal or non-work related? Would it be a good thing to ban this completely?

Who rings me just to catch up with gossip? What proportion of my overall time on the phone is focussed on things that make a difference?

Are there people who ask my opinion more because they are lazy than because they really value it?

What kind of communication should I have with the people who work for me? What is the split between information and motivation? What are their expectations?

How often does my boss need an update? What level of detail is needed? What is the best communication channel (face to face, email, phone call, post it note?)

Answer these questions and you will have taken the first important step to allocating your time, which is assessing the criteria for communication.

Who's in control?

Your boss has a dull monotone voice, wanders off the subject all the time and has no idea how to control the flow of an agenda, so why would you want to go to his weekly meeting? It can only be because he/she expects you to be there.

This illustrates the issue of control. You may have decided who you want to communicate with and the most efficient channels but you have to take account of the other party too.

You can use this matrix to plot your planning.

Low control	High control	
		Important and relevant
Grin and bear it, you really need this stuff	Make the most of it	
Make an attempt to manage as well as you can	Get rid Jettison Eject Quit	Trivial and irrelevant

Take some action

In the areas of high control you should be thinking about how you can make the most of the opportunities you have. Are you really using your time well, is there a way of shortening meetings, could you add other elements to make them more interesting to more participants.

Equally when it comes to decisions about what you get rid of you can afford to be brutal, it's within your control.

Much more difficult to manage are the areas of low control. Your boss probably won't take too kindly to being told his meetings are pointless, but that doesn't mean you should give up altogether. Maybe your peers feel the same and over time you might, with gentle persuasion and coercion, be able to bring about some changes.

Target

You now know how you feel about elements of the communication mix that you want to improve upon. Also, you have made some free time and had another reminder of the practical things that work for you and the ones that don't.

From this you need to target 3 areas for improvement, taking into account both **action** and **frequency**.

This initial scheme will drive how much further planning you need to do because if you choose 3 simple actions that only need to be implemented once then you will have fulfilled the plan, after which, you need to start again. Remember what Russell Grossman said at the beginning of the chapter if you need convincing, if you don't keep moving forward, you will be left behind!

Some things might take longer to implement and there may be an ongoing commitment, which eats into some of your time on a weekly or even daily basis.

Here are some examples of actions you might think about. See how the frequency affects the overall level of commitment you have to make.

I am going to improve my presentation skills by enrolling on a public speaking course at college.

I am going to spend the last 30 minutes of the working day tidying the email inbox, managing incoming mail into files and deleting any redundant messages.

I am going to source one new trade magazine, industry publication, newspaper or periodical per week with information relevant to my job. Then I'm going to take one hour per week to read and digest the publication, taking notes on content and learning as appropriate.

I am going to email all my friends who send me junk mail or jokes and ask them to redirect future messages to my home account.

I am going to use my voicemail only when really necessary.

I am going to restrict all my team meetings to a maximum of one hour and produce an agenda in advance.

If there are dozens of things you want to achieve and you're afraid you're only tackling a few then remember that this isn't a one-off process. You're just choosing the highest priorities and the more progress you make with them, the sooner you'll be able to move onto other issues.

For the time being you can afford to be adventurous in your thinking and take some risks in this safe environment, after all until you reach the implementation stage it's only you who is being affected by the decisions. Look at the next section and you'll get some idea of what will be needed to help you achieve your objectives, if it looks too daunting then come up with more manageable targets.

Resourcing

The final part of the planning process is to look at how you are actually going to carry out the plan.

What are the resources you'll need to deliver your objectives? This might be a combination of physical items, as in the earlier case of the trade magazines, or you may need the help of colleagues, if you like, your *human* resources.

Here's a final checklist in this chapter to help spark your ideas.

Will I need to retrain? Who can help with that?

How and where can I source the physical items I need? (consider logistics, cost, sharing the resources with others)

What research tools are available (internet, internal documentation etc.)

When will I know that I'm making progress, what milestones can I put in place?

Is there anyone who I can turn to as a mentor?

Who are my role models?

Assessment

With five minutes left of your planning hour you should be taking time to look back at the process. This is simply to check that you managed to do what you promised.

Have you successfully audited your current position?

Do you know what kind of communicator you are and where your weaknesses lie?

Are the time-wasting activities now apparent?

Have you thought which ones you can jettison?

Have you been able to come up with some objectives that are achievable?

Are there some actions set against each of them?

Have you identified who and what can help, as well as considering things like cost, timescale and logistics?

If you've achieved only 75% of this, you will still have a workable plan. There will be things you can be getting on with right away. Rather than worrying about the remaining 25%, use the last minute of your hour to diary some more planning time within the next month. Think about where the gaps are and jot a few notes down about how you'd like to fill them in your next planning session (it might mean gathering some resources in the intervening period).

Now that you've finished you can tick your planning phase off the list and start on implementation.

Top tips for better planning

Plan to plan, if you don't it won't happen.

Do it quickly. Keep it focussed. That way you'll remember it better and it won't be nearly so painful.

Planning is dull, achievement is enjoyable. So see planning as part of the process of achieving a shift in your skills.

You can only feel good about your plan if you believe in it.

At any one time you can only wear one pair of shoes, concentrate on the task in hand and get round to the others later.

Apply an elevator test to your plan. Could you describe it to a colleague in a few short sentences?

Construct a planning cycle that includes time for review and reflection.

Write it down, pin it up. Keep the fact that you have a plan to achieve at the front of your mind, even if you have to attach it to the fridge door.

A planning example

Shooting a video

How much planning would you put into the shooting of a short video for your next company conference?

Say the CEO wants to present a piece to camera, followed by footage of the manufacturing plant and then some customers buying the end product.

You're working alongside the producer who will cover all the technical and creative aspects, but between you, you need to plan the logistics.

Here are a few things you might have to consider; the length of the final piece and overall cost, which budget lines are essential and which just 'nice-to-have', availability of the CEO, a location which is quiet and fit for purpose, access to the manufacturing plant, health and safety issues, production insurance, permission to film customers, how and where to edit your footage, what format to produce it on?

All of this is just scratching the surface. There will be many more things to consider before you are ready to start 'shooting'.

With a 'glamorous' piece of communication like video it is tempting to jump ahead, straight to the point when the camera starts to roll, but you can already start to see how much pre-work has to go on in order to deliver the finished product.

If you logged all the hours needed to complete the project you would find that between half and two thirds would be taken in the planning and preparation stages.

The bigger the communication the greater the need is to plan. In the case of the video taking short cuts will at best result in an inferior product, or at worst the collapse of the project all together.

Try this

Planning is an example of an activity that is best tackled quickly using maximum concentration. None of us can sustain this kind of intense working across a whole day.

Under these circumstances you have to prepare yourself to make sure you achieve what you set out. The first thing is to put a time limit on the period of concentration (good teachers don't sustain the same activity for more than 20 minutes without some kind of break, we wouldn't recommend more than an hour on any one task).

Next, make sure there can be no distractions, firstly from the things we've mentioned like phones ringing and people calling by your office, but also you need to be clear-headed. It's no good sitting down to intense activity if there is an important and urgent task hanging over you.

Stay alert and focussed.

Big plans and daily plans

Now you've looked at your overall communication strategy and drawn up a plan to keep it on track. The difficulty will be sustaining this on a daily basis when faced with all the other tasks that have to be done.

Lots of people fail because they don't have a daily plan.

Making a things-to-do list is a good start, but if you have no sense of priority it's of little use. To be really effective we need to build in two additional factors. Firstly we need to put a time allocation next to each item, otherwise how will we ever know if there are enough hours in the day to do what must be done? This time allocation should be in the form of ten-minute time slots (there's not much you can do in less than ten minutes), and you shouldn't have any task that is more than an hour.

If you have a huge project that will take many hours to complete, allocate one-hour time slots to it, calling each a different thing as in this way you will feel a greater sense of achievement that you have moved further towards completing it.

Next, put a number next to each item so that you have a chronological order to follow. In doing this you should balance the tasks against each other, so if you have a period of intense concentration, you should then do something that is less taxing. Don't be afraid to include routine tasks on the list, they still take up your valuable time.

Here's an example of a structured things-to-do list:

1. Re-list tasks (1)
5. Check hotel availability for Thursday (1)
3. Prep production meeting report (2)
4. Write production meeting report (3)
7. Email Emma re: costings (1)
6. Reply to Ben with suggestions of agenda items (3)
10. Research competitor activity online (6)
9. Send thank you note to the team (2)
8. Write up meeting report for M.D. (6)
2. Sort and action incoming post (2)
11. Sort and action email inbox (2)

The number down the right hand side is the length of time (in ten minute units) that you have allocated to each task, so there's an hour for the research activity, but only 20 minutes to sort out the post. This isn't an exact science, yes, you can decide that you're only going to spend half an hour writing up the production meeting report, but you have no idea what's in your email inbox. Over time you will get better at predicting how much each item will need, but if you set yourself just 20 minutes to clear the email it's surprising how much it focusses your mind.

Most people's levels of concentration are higher in the morning so you should plan to do the difficult tasks then.

In between the heavy stuff, like the report writing you have allowed yourself either a reward, (saying thank you to the team is a good thing to do and will make you feel better as a people manager), or what we'd call mindless tasks, like checking the hotel availability for example. They take very little concentration but allow you a break of sorts.

Incidentally you are allowed proper breaks for a coffee or lunch as well!

To recap, there are three stages to making your list. Firstly, write down the tasks to be done, next allocate a time frame (in ten minute segments), then finally, number the list in the order you will take things.

One final word on the way you allocate your time, it's good to make a habit of repetitive tasking. Remember the production line technique we mentioned earlier, originally pioneered by the Ford Motor Company? If you do all of the same type of thing one after another you get into a rhythm, which increases efficiency. It's much better than hopping from one thing to another. Just remember to build in a balance so that you don't go mad with the monotony.

According to...

Professor Cary Cooper

'You should start every day with a things-to-do list.

I ask myself what's really important today and I put it in priority order, then I look at everything that comes in throughout the day both electronic and hard copy and I decide if any of these things should change my list. If the answer is no then you leave it to the side and get on with your list. If something comes in that is really vital and supersedes your list items then you put it in'.

Try this

Get hold of an extra A4 size diary for your things-to-do lists.

This has a number of benefits. Firstly it's great for medium and longer term planning as you can flick ahead through the diary and put tasks in for a day, a week or even several months hence. That's particularly useful for setting aside conscious planning time at regular intervals.

Also you'll be better able to track your progress through tasks by looking back to see how many you get through in an average day. Over time, your daily plans will get more efficient as you become more accurate in allocating time slots to different functions.

Finally, it'll shame you into doing the things you hate but are part of your job. This is because you transfer any incomplete tasks forward each day and the constant reminder of the things you put off should prompt you into action.

If you're really smart you'll put in all the family birthdays too!

The Elevator Test for Chapter 12

- Planning is the first step to achieving our goals
- Short intense bursts of planning make it less of a chore
- Time is both finite and valuable – be careful how you allocate it
- Make your objectives manageable and give yourself a chance of hitting your targets

■ Get into the daily habit of making a prioritised, time-allocated, things-to-do list

■ Try to allocate the most difficult tasks to the morning, leaving the afternoon for less taxing routine

CHAPTER 13

Six strategies

Where do we go from here?

Now you know what the panel of experts thinks, you've digested the theory of better communication, you've even set out a plan for the future, all that's left is a reminder of what you'll need to help carry it out.

This final chapter summarises the learning of the six most important points in the book.

Think about your audience

Whether it's a room full of expectant faces waiting for you to impart some vital information or a chat with a junior colleague at the coffee machine, you need to pay equal attention and respect to where they are coming from.

Try to actively listen and get a real understanding of the motivations, aspirations and fears of the other party.

Consider their ideals, their lifestyle, job function, background and prejudices; be sensitive to their view of you.

Convey conviction

None of us is right all of the time, but we earn great respect from people if we can truly convince them that we have belief in our ideas.

If you think something is right then say so, with passion. With experience you can learn to harness the power of that passion.

Try to make sure you keep your arguments well-founded in logic and back them with the zeal that you really feel.

This conviction is a very powerful persuader and you can carry people along with you on a wave of enthusiasm. Be sure that you keep an eye on your goals and make everyone aware when you've achieved them, so that they get to experience for themselves the benefits of conviction.

One thing's certain, if you don't feel passionate about what you're doing, you're in trouble; no one is going to follow you if they think you are half-hearted about the job in hand.

It is impossible to sustain any kind of enthusiasm for an idea you don't agree with.

'Shut up and listen'

Resist the urge to rush in with your own opinion until you've heard the facts. Which of us hasn't at some time lost our temper, only to find that the subject of our anger is actually a failing on our part? There is nothing more humbling than blaming someone else for failure, only to find that it's our fault.

So it is with communication.

It's much easier to formulate ideas that are acceptable if we've listened to the other party first. Try too to resist the temptation to simply *appear* attentive, instead make the effort to really hear what the other person is saying and meaning.

Stay conscious – think and plan

Don't drift along taking things as they come. Your planning should have helped you do this, but it's really easy to see that as a 'once-only' exercise and it is precisely that attitude, which stops us from continually assessing where we're up to.

It'll help if you book more planning time in a physical sense by blocking it out in your diary, but also on a daily basis try to take five minutes before you go home to think about what you've achieved with your communication. Were you clear from the start about your purpose? Did people get the message? How well did you manage incoming communication, how efficient were you?

At an even more detailed level, do a spot check every now and then on how you handled a phone call, whether your reply to an email was efficient and economical without being cold, if you made the points you wanted to at a meeting.

The great thing about being conscious of all these things is that it gives us the freedom and the power to make choices. We decide the best use of our own time and in doing so free ourselves up from the effects of other people's poor communication or planning.

The flip side is when we take things as they come, then others are making choices for us, they're filling our inbox, allocating us tasks, getting their own way, the result is energy-sapping and unfulfilling. Remember, stay conscious, actively conscious.

Be sensitive to culture

This takes the job of understanding your audience a step further. You're not just responding to the group of individuals within your vicinity, but in the wider environment. It's important to see this both on a company and international level, so as you move from one organisation to another, try and pick up on the differences quickly. If you're transported to another part of the world it's even more vital that you understand custom and practice.

Use your listening skills and ask lots of questions. You'll be forgiven for a genuine mistake, but not for cultural arrogance, if you make it appear that yours is the 'right' way, simply because of where you're from.

Recognise the importance of storytelling

From an early age stories play an important part in our lives, but the tales we hear in childhood aren't just there to amuse us, they pass on important messages that define the society we live in. They are our first experience of the triumph of good over evil, of what's right and wrong.

Maybe the most significant part of storytelling is the way it embeds a message in our memory, so that we can recount the learning many years later.

In business, a good story can have the same effect with some added benefits. It can remove the attention from us as the story-teller and place it on the characters; they then become the expert or the fall guy. Conversely, when we want to, we can use it to focus attention on ourselves and make us the 'victim' of the story, which is something many skilled communicators do to show they are vulnerable and to develop empathy with their audience.

Think about the stories you already know, make a conscious effort to collect more as you go along and practise telling them in a safe environment (to friends in a social situation or to a couple of colleagues over a coffee), before you use them as the pivotal point of a major presentation.

These are the strategies we think are important, they draw on the experience of all our contributors and will go a long way to making your communication persuasive, understandable and well-respected. Most of all it will make other people want to communicate back and that is at the core of all successful business.

Our last piece of advice is this.

Be yourself. You had an opportunity earlier in the book to find out a bit more about who you are, use that knowledge and your natural personality, combine it with what you have read and enjoy more successful communication.

Appendix I
Further Recommended Reading

Argyle, M. (1967), *The Psychology of Interpersonal Behaviour*. London: Penguin Books

Christie, B. (1981), *Face to File Communication*. Chichester: John Wiley & Sons.

Clutterbuck, D. and Hirst, S. (2002), *Talking Business: Making Communication Work*. Oxford: Butterworth-Heinemann.

Covey, S. (1999), *The 7 Habits of Highly Effective People*. New York: Simon & Schuster.

Dive, B. (2002), *The Healthy Organization*. London: Kogan Page.

Goleman, D. (1998), *Working with Emotional Intelligence*. London: Bloomsbury.

Grout, J. and Perrin, S. (2002), *Recruiting Excellence*. London: McGraw Hill.

Haslam, C. and Bryman, A. (1994), *Social Scientists Meet the Media*. London: Routledge.

Kline, N. (1998), *Time to Think*. London: Cassell Illustrated.

Seeley, M. and Hargreaves, G. (2003), *Managing in the Email Office*. Oxford: Butterworth-Heinemann.

Smith, P. B. and Bond, M. (1993), *Social Psychology Across Cultures*. Brighton: Harvester Press.

John Akers – Manager of the Birmingham Office of the National Family Mediation Service – also acts as a Relationship Counsellor for Relate

Simon Armson – Former Chief Executive of The Samaritans

Chris Brewster – Professor of International Human Resource Management at South Bank University in London

Michael Broadbent – Director of Corporate Affairs at HSBC Bank

David Clutterbuck – Visiting Professor at Sheffield Hallam University

Cary Cooper – Distinguished Professor of Organisational Psychology at Lancaster University Management School

Bill Dalton – Former CEO of HSBC Bank

Keith Edelman – Former Managing Director of Arsenal F.C. and former Chief Executive of Storehouse PLC

Val Gooding – Former CEO of BUPA

Russell Grossman – Head of Internal Communications at the BBC

Keith Harris – Chairman of Seymour Pierce Group Plc and former Chairman of the Football League

Derek Hatton – former Labour politician, now a Broadcaster and Motivational Speaker

Surinder Hundal – HR and Internal Communications Director of Nokia

Chris Lewis – founder and CEO Chris Lewis PR

Lynn Rutter – Change Manager, Global HR Projects, Oxfam

Kevin Roberts – Saatchi and Saatchi Worldwide CEO

Chris Major – Head of PR at AstraZeneca

Peter Sanguinetti – former Director of Corporate Communications, British Gas

Jan Shawe – Director of Corporate Communications, Sainsbury's Supermarkets Limited

Doug Simkiss – Consultant Paediatrician at the Birmingham Community Children's Centre

Alistair Smith – Chairperson of Alite Ltd a company which specialises in development work in and around the fields of motivation, teaching and learning

Simon Terrington – founding director of Human Capital, a consultancy that advises media companies on their creative strategies

Kay Winsper – Head of Great Company at Microsoft